Essentially

BEING ME IN A BECOMING WORLD

Pauline Aweto

Grosvenor House
Publishing Limited

This book is published by
Grosvenor House Publishing Ltd
Link House
140 The Broadway, Tolworth, Surrey, KT6 7HT.
www.grosvenorhousepublishing.co.uk

A CIP record for this book
is available from the British Library

ISBN 978-1-80381-596-1
eBook ISBN 978-1-80381-605-0

To the glory of God and the salvation of souls.

Dedication

To Phoenix Chioma-Rose Hambrook Eze and Aurora Chika-Mae Hambrook Eze for adding meaning and purpose to my journey.

Acknowledgments

My gratitude goes to God, the Author of my life, being, and becoming, for making it possible for me to share my reflections in this book.

I am immensely grateful to my mother, Mrs Theresa Aweto, for her pioneering and exemplary practice of the Christian faith, which has greatly influenced me.

I thank my sister and friend, Mrs Felicia Aghwadoma for her inspiration of boundless generosity and faith in action.

I am equally grateful to my sons, Chris, and Ken, for the joys of motherhood. I particularly thank Chris, for allowing me to publish some of his letters in this book, and to use our common platform of vulnerability to heal others.

Finally, I thank you, my readers, who through the contents and experiences I share in this book, will be empowered, and inspired to maximise the potential of who you have been created and called to be. Essentially.

Other titles by Pauline Aweto

The Sound of Silence

The Changing Landscape of Christianity in Africa

Wartime Rape: African Values at Crossroads

TABLE OF CONTENTS

PART I

BEING ME

1

Memories from Childhood

The middle name I was given at birth was connected to the circumstances surrounding my triumphant entry into the Aweto family. I was the 5th consecutive girl in the order of arrival. I knew my father more in death than in life. I was barely thirteen when he passed. He was not the type of father to decree, petition or even command God for a male child while I was still being carefully knitted together in my mother's womb. He was a Christian, a Catholic to the core. His relationship with God defined his very existence, his being, doing, having and even dying. His attitude to God was that of gratitude. His children were gifts from divine providence. He didn't have the luxury of asking God to consult him to know the sex of the child he wanted. His God was not a transactional God. But the time was what it was. To be fair, things have not changed for the better since then. Most African men still prefer male children. One was never enough. Exactly as it was, when I was born.

"Owhobeno" was my middle name.

Literarily, "unpredictable".

My father probably envisaged that with education, a girl child like me, would be as valuable as a male child. It was as if, with this middle name, he wanted to make a statement. He wanted to tell the world to "watch this space", to "watch this girl" to see what she would become.

I came back from school one day to meet my maternal grandmother. She wanted to know why I sobbed hysterically.

At school, I'd found out that a girl in my class had my middle name as her surname. As a child, I didn't understand why I had to bear the same name as a full-grown male adult. My grandmother had to change my middle name to the one I currently use. Thinking about this years later, I believe the middle name given to me by my father was the one more applicable to the person I have become.

I grew up at a time when children, especially the girl child, were not allowed to have dreams and aspirations. As children, we were either awake or asleep and nothing in-between. When we were awake, we simply played the days away. We enjoyed every bit of it like there was no tomorrow. Bedtime came at the end of an extremely productive play-day. Our little bodies simply gave way to the forces of nature, rewarding us with the undeserved rest we needed to start and finish another day.

Questions about what we would become in the near or distant future were taboos. Boys grew up, groomed to become men and heads of families and households. They learnt a trade, acquired skills, or even went to school to prepare them for the life ahead. It wasn't so for the girl child. The society limited her aspirations to becoming a wife and progressively a mother. This was a-no- choice-matter of natural sequence.

Like every child of my time, I was just happy to be alive. I lived every day of my childhood with the energy of a child in a carefree and somewhat innocent world, where morality and the knowledge of what was right and just were simply everyone's business. It was the norm. There were only few exceptions to the rule, if there were any.

My mother didn't need to read my bedtime stories or sing a lullaby to make me fall asleep. She couldn't have, even if she had wanted to. It was not part of her job description as a mother. I was often too tired to be afraid of bad dreams or nightmares that would have sent me to my parents' room. It was an off-limit locum. I was only allowed in when I was in trouble and my mother had the mission to execute a private monologue.

In such instances, there was absolutely no room for me to explain or justify my actions. This was never part of the bargain. Just a pair of listening ears was all that was required. And a pair of eyes that never dared to look up, explain or complain.

Often these monologues were not always about what I did wrong but where I went wrong. I was liable to judgement just by being in the wrong place or in the wrong companion of people. People who, according to my parents' judgement were most likely to have negative influence on me. I was too young to understand but that didn't matter. Sometimes, it was because I was carried away or overplayed. At other times it was because I wasn't conscious of time and didn't return home on time. Most of the time once was more than enough to break the golden rule and face the consequences for a long time to come. Some of these consequences remained immortalised in the memory compartment of my soul. I needed to remember the last time it happened so that it doesn't happen, ever again. This was the only way I demonstrated my "*mea colpa*". This never-again resolution was, personally for me, a dogma, which remained unquestionable, only to be embraced, even if I didn't understand. As a child, I wasn't just not expected to understand, I had to accept everything in good faith, especially when they came from infallible parents as mine.

I remember when another child in the neighbourhood visited us. She was on her way to an errand, with a three-pence copper coin. My sister, Feli and I got so carried away as we built castles in the sand and hid the three-pence copper coin in it. The whole idea was an impromptu competition to find out who will be the lucky one to recover the coin from the heap of sand. To our greatest nightmare, the coin was never again found. Our friend cried despairingly, not knowing what to tell her mother about what happened to the coin and why her mission was unaccomplished even before it began. My sister and I were doubly ill-fated. We had both broken the Aweto code of conduct. We were in the wrong place at the wrong time. Our father, the "Teacher" as my mother (fondly and respectfully) called him, and the "Catechist" (as he was known in the village), was at home. This was by some strange design. But this was not all. My elder brother now retired Professor Aweto was also visiting at the time. He had come home for a break from the ivory tower. As far as I can remember, this was the only time I saw him visiting. The next time was when he came home at the news of my father's passing.

My sister and I knew what we were in for. There was no guessing at what awaited us. However, I was less fortunate than she was. There was a stark difference between us. We handled pain and other forms of physical chastisement or corporal punishment differently.

On this occasion, my father chose a bundle of broomsticks to teach us the lesson that we have not forgotten, more than half a century on. He must have made this choice in consideration of the providential visit of my brother who assisted him in picking up the sticks of broom that were not caught up in our feeble flesh, tied them up and handed them back to him in a conspiracy of absolute silence.

My sister was first in line to receive the consequential rewards of our inaction. My own agony was further protracted and doubled. I watched my sister and passively experienced her pain as a precursor to what awaited me in a matter of time. The lesson I learnt was also double. I absorbed, at my own expense that I must have a mind of my own. It was not justifiable for me to simply follow my sister, who was a handful of years older than me. I appraised that people who are older, who should know better, can't be used to excuse my participation. I learnt individual responsibility and accountability for my actions.

Not being in the wrong place at the wrong time continues to be one of my guiding principles in life. I thought this was all about my parents being too strict and not giving us the same opportunity to have fun as other children of our age. It was part of the "Aweto-ness". I was constantly reminded of who I was. I was the daughter of a disciplinarian and a community teacher. I would give anything for my double blessing to have ended here. But this was not the case, fortunately, or unfortunately. He was also a Catechist. He was one of the few who understood and spoke the language of the "white man", the missionary priest. He also simultaneously interpreted his sermons, which he delivered, in the very language of God himself, in the English language.

My Father, Mr Anthony Idigun Aweto

2

A Daughter of Difference

One very special privilege I enjoyed as the daughter of a Catechist was receiving my first Holy Communion in a very early morning mass, attended by a very few. It must have been at about 5.30. At the time, it felt like 3am. I was too anxious to sleep the night before. It was one of the few times that I went somewhere alone with my father. Between the awe and holy fear of receiving the body of Christ for the first time and going to Church alone with my father, I didn't know which I dreaded more.

I rode with my father for the first time on his new Raleigh bicycle. It was also the only time and the last time. He wasn't a man of pleasantries. He didn't bother about political correctness or gender sensitivity. To him, I was just a child who must make the next step after baptism, to receive the sacrament of the Holy Eucharist. This was all that mattered. He had two priorities: to get me to Church and to get me there earlier than Fr Brown who, apart from speaking the language of God, also kept to time, like the angel of death. As children, we thought Fr Brown was a spitting image of God himself. Most images we had of Jesus, or the saints depicted them as supernatural and transcendent beings. They were so far away, so totally different, and so white. Fr Brown seldom walked on our dusty streets. He often drove his white Volkswagen Beetles that raised dust, reminding people to quicken their steps not to be late for mass. As children, we felt there was something magical about Fr Brown. The few times we spotted him walking, we felt it was Jesus walking on the sea. Fr Brown had dentures. He scared the death out of us each time he took them out of his mouth or moved them in his mouth. For Fr Brown, this was the only way he got rid of the dozens of half-naked and bare-footed children who shouted "*Oyinbo*" after him. For the children, this was even a greater miracle than Jesus's turning water into wine. Nothing could be more miraculous and mysterious.

Back to that special morning of my first Holy Communion, my father made me sit on his "male" designed bicycle. I sat with both legs on either side of the hard pole which connected the front wheel to the back. To be fair, that was the only provision for a potential passenger, male or female. There was no due consideration for my yet to emerge gender. I was a child and that was it. The "female" qualification was still somewhere in the making. It was definitely not in the mind of my father.

With the spinning of the spokes, my *via crucis* was elevated to 360 degrees and more. My father rode majestically at a five mile per hour speed. In my thoughts, this was eternally suicidal. The journey of twenty minutes or even less seemed endless like one of twenty years. As painful as the journey was, it was also the most privileged time I came closest to him. From this experience I started internalising what I would later on study in my first year of Philosophy as the existence of opposites; how both pain and pleasure co-exist and sometimes co-die; how it was necessary to experience both and how one is meaningless without the other; how joy can only be understood and defined in the context of sadness, in the same way as light could only be fully comprehended in darkness, and how each one has to give way to the other, in timeless and seamless transition as the circle of life continued.

My father's practice as a teacher and disciplinarian by default started from home. My older siblings who were fortunate enough to attend the same school where he taught, were equally unfortunate enough to be punished twice, if necessary, from a teacher and then a father. He disciplined us for specific acts and this, to a large extent defined his choice of instrument. He often used the cane. He never raised his hands against any of his students, children or my mother. We received punishments for what we did wrong, real, or imagined, like the day my sister and I were guilty of being in the wrong place at the wrong time. Then we were simply witnesses in an event that could potentially have labelled us as thieves. My father couldn't live with that.

I also learnt a life-changing lesson on one Sunday morning. This was before I was ten. My father was officiating at the morning Church service. There was no priest at that time to say mass. Priests then were an uncommon specie. They were mainly Irish priests with a handful of indigenous clergymen. Most future priests then were still being churned in the major seminary. The format of the Church service conducted by catechists like my father was very different. There were hymns, ancient and modern, prayers, litanies, and then readings from the old and new testaments. This was followed by the gospel and a short explanation by the officiating minister, a Catechist or Church elder.

My mother had to return home from Church, for some unexplainable reasons. The day's business was yet inconclusive then. She realised she didn't have the house keys. She sent me back to the Church to fetch them from my father. He was still at the altar. I went straight to him to deliver the message from my mother. He was reading a text in the English language and simultaneously translating it into the local language to the congregation as if he was reading in the local dialect itself. I had watched him at home prepare, rehearse, repeat and study for his presentations. He never took anything by chance. He rigorously prepared what he was going to say and chose the right words to use. He never sought the aid of a dictionary. He always reflected, read, meditated and sourced for better words and ways to best deliver the message to the congregation. Somehow, he always found the right translations or used pronunciations similar to the original word in a tone that communicated meaning with clarity. When this failed, and it seldom did, he resorted to explanatory and descriptive analysis that still conveyed the intended message.

I stood there.

These were the longest minutes that defied the sixty second rule. I waited for him to ask me what I wanted. In my family's unwritten code of conduct, it was usual not to speak until we were spoken to or asked to speak. On the other hand, my father expected me to use my own initiative. He expected me to understand that it was the wrong place and the wrong time for me to ask him anything. Even if it were a matter of life or death. No place was more sacred and dreadful as the altar. It was even more dreadful when my father officiated. I stood beside him, immobile as a stationary truck for who knows how long. I struggled to remain in that position. I felt like I was between a rock and a hard surface. I couldn't fathom which I feared the more. Was it the congregation whose investigative spirits I discerned from afar? Was it rather my own father, who resisted to continue uninterruptedly? It must have been extremely difficult for him to ignore me. One thing about him was his profound sense of duty and commitment to the affairs of God and the Church. The same was true about his work as a teacher. He gave his 100% attention. He was incapable of being distracted, even by a ten-year-old daughter who stood motionless beside him while he delivered the message of God from God.

My misery came to a climax, when he looked at me, but this was not my main concern. It must have been the only time my eyes met with his. It felt like a sword had pierced my soul, more than a double-edged sword. He was a man of few words. His silence often said it all. This time, it was ear-splitting.

I lived with my father for no more than 10 years. These were long enough for him to have established the rock-solid foundation upon which my entire life, principles and values were anchored. From him, I learnt discipline, in principle and in practice. I absorbed routine as second nature and made the commitment to duty and obligations my breastplate. He imparted a sense of pride and dignity in me as an individual, in the first place, and then a child of God. He did not exclude me, as a girl child from education, at a time when it was not profitable for parents to invest in the education of their girls. This was his greatest gift to me. Education gave me the wings to fly, to be the best I can ever be, to embrace my individuality as a person and further down the line, as a woman, to be me, unapologetically.

One of the rare traits I inherited from my father is organisational ability. He never left anything to chance. He was a master planner. Having ten children appeared like they just 'came' but he had planned for all of them to attend boarding schools. He meticulously chose boys-only or girls-only schools, as against mixed-sex schools. He didn't settle for the convenience of nearby schools. I later found out that he specifically refused to contribute to the building of the village secondary school as he intentionally didn't want his children to receive their education there. It was a choice he made and defended without having to justify himself to others.

Ironically after he had passed on, it became necessary for me to come back home to attend the same local secondary school, for the convenience of keeping my young- widowed mother company. Subsequently, all other siblings after me attended the same secondary school.

One unique practice my father instituted in his family made him stand out as a man above and beyond his time. As a father of six girls, the general expectation was that he would use his daughters to create wealth for himself by asking for extortionate bride price payments from the potential husbands of his daughters. He was different from other fathers who asked for significantly high prices as if their daughters were being sold to the highest bidder. He made the conscious and ground-breaking decision to impose a symbolic token of a few shillings. The statement he made by this singular act was that his daughters were not for sale.

He took another step further – he made sure all his girls received education, at a time when the slogan was "Women's Education Ends in Kitchen" (WEEK). He was never in a hurry to marry off his girls and pass on the responsibility to their husbands. He was, essentially, forward thinking and innovative in his approach. He unconsciously advocated for the empowerment of women through education. He didn't want his daughters to end up as liabilities to their husbands. He envisaged his daughters as well-educated wives and mothers with career potentials in their chosen fields, contributing to their families, without being confined to the domestic walls alone.

Reflectively, maybe this was one of the reasons why none of us was ever a victim of domestic violence in our relationships, past and present. This might just be a simple coincidence, but in digging deeper into the roots of domestic violence, factors related to the huge financial pressure men had to be put through in 'paying' for their life partners could be confirmed as significantly correlating.

The awareness that my father accepted me as a person and didn't wish I was a male shaped my identity and sense of pride as an individual. Nothing mattered after that. Consequently, I have always believed that I am made of much more and made for much more, beyond my gender identity or classification.

As Awetos, there were things we were just not expected to do or even think of. There were places we were not expected to visit or seen at. I remember there was an annual festival that attracted visitors from across the country to my village. It was taboo for us to watch the parade as it went past the front of our house which was located right in the centre of the village and in very close vicinity to the central shrine, which was the main point of focus during this festival. As children we were made to dread this event. As Christians we were made to hide so that pictures of us would not appear in this "evil" celebration, which could be used as evidence against us on the last day and prevent us from gaining access to heaven. Nothing could be more frightful than that for the feeble mind of a child who believed everything, literarily.

Many years on, although the initial fear instilled in me remain, I understood that the festival was simply fetish, a pagan practice but part of the village's cultural and unique identity. This was when Christianity was not all- penetrating as it is now. One hundred years after Catholicism was first introduced into the village, the practice goes on, but it is no longer as popular as it used to be. Fewer and fewer people participate or even visit.

My Mother, Mrs Theresa Iritevwobo Aweto

3

Conversations with My Mother

I come from a culture where silence is golden. Many things are left unsaid, often, better imagined. Many questions remained unasked until it becomes impossible to find answers, as people carry them away with them as eternal secrets to their graves. I have lived most of my life away from my mother. This made me hunger more for some answers, which our time apart over the years has denied me. As a mother, myself, there were instances when my children asked me questions that I honestly couldn't answer. This stirred in me, the desire to find the courage to ask my mother some burning questions

I'm not ashamed to say that my mother's memory is a dozen time better than mine. I haven't been able to find out why. I tried to find explanations in the fact that I'm able to commit my thoughts to pen and paper, "empty" the contents of my memory in order not to forget them and to make space for more. I'm sometimes tempted to believe that my memory has a limited capacity, some terabytes at the maximum. This is quite contrary for my mother, who is specially gifted with a very high-pitched memory. Sometimes, I felt really humbled when she reminded me of things I should have remembered but have forgotten.

In recent years, I have formed the habit of spending most of my annual leave holidays with her. In 2021 when she clocked 90, I decided to embark on a fact-finding mission that lasted for five uninterrupted weeks. It was a unique opportunity I had and wanted to utilise it to the maximum.

I'd prepared my questions beforehand – almost nothing was off-limits. I specifically wanted to know about my father and their relationship. She has practically been living her entire life in memory of him. She could have remarried and enjoyed marital benefits or at least sought the companionship of another man. I also wanted to know why all ten of us were so different. Inevitably (this is the hardest part), I wanted to know how she felt about transiting to the great beyond or if she had any regrets at all.

From our conversations, I made a very significant discovery about my Catholic origin, which, until then, I'd believed I inherited from my father's family. Contrarily, I learnt that both my grandmother and great-grand mother were Catholics. Although it was shocking for me to discover that my father was a convert, it gave me great joy to know that I'm a fourth generation Catholic, from the lineage of women. It was quite a revelation to hear my mother recount all she had to go through just to receive a Catholic wedding. They had to travel an equivalence of sixty miles or more on foot to reach and return from the nearest Catholic Church with a residing priest (Irish) who alone could celebrate this sacrament. They had to make the same journey twice, as the priest was absent during their first visit.

From my mother, I learnt that my father was a life-long learner, who also sought continuous professional and personal development, even as the father of a young growing family. The children, coming in, one after the other, didn't deter him from seeking further knowledge to improve himself. Sometimes, my mother had to leave my siblings with my grandparents and great grandparents to join or visit him in his place of study. To a large extent, this accounted for the different villages where we were born and by extension, the different personalities we all developed which were not homogenous.

Most importantly, I discovered that my father was the midwife who delivered her of all her children. He must have been a man who lived far beyond and above his generation. It was very unusual, even today, for men to be present at such an event. He was a non-conformist and I certainly inherited a great dose from him.

Reverend Sr Pauline Aweto, Rome 1987

4

Life at First Choice

At the time I was growing up, choice was a word that was absent from our vocabulary and mental dictionaries. There were simply no options or other possibilities to consider. The absence of choice meant different things to different people. Some didn't have options in terms of what they ate or wore, the Churches they worshipped or the schools they attended. At that time in my village, there were only two Churches, two primary schools and a secondary school. These were the Catholic and Baptist Churches and primary schools. Children who were Catholics ended up in Catholic schools and those whose parents were Baptists, simply went to the Baptist school. Today, these are still the only schools in my village, but the Churches have increased exponentially to forty and above. At the time it was more of the available becoming desirable. Chance was more applicable to individual circumstances than choice.

One choice however, was that between good and evil. Everyone seemed to have known what the right thing was and simply did it. There were also not many households. Each family prided itself in its name, which everyone in that family tried to protect, by doing the right thing. The Awetos were not in any way different. More also, because my father was an educator and a catechist, my family was more of a model family. The great expectation was that we all had the moral code of conduct written in our DNA. If an action was considered prohibited for others, for the Awetos, it was non-negotiable. It felt like we were pencils without erasers.

Essentially, we all lived in the village like one big family. We knew each other. Doing good and being kind was the norm. The contrary was the exception, which was rather rare. Educating children and correcting them was every adult's duty. This was not left exclusively to their parents. Everyone lived in harmony, respect and acceptance of differences in religious, pagan or traditional beliefs. One unifying factor was sound and undiluted moral judgement. One common good was social harmony.

Ovu Grammar School was the only secondary school in my village. It had no religious affiliations. The first principal was an Irish Catholic priest. This added moral flavour to the enrichment of the school's curriculum as well as exclusive practice. Like my own father, the Principal was a disciplinarian. Many politicians and rich parents sent their children to this school for the benefits of discipline, academic excellence and the dream of their children raised in the straight and narrow corridors of the zeal of a young expatriate priest. This was aided by a boarding facility, which made it desirable for their children to receive an all-round education. This included moral education, and a quasi-ascetic life in a remote village. It had only one major tarred road that extended from its beginning to the end. Students were unexposed to the temptations and enticements of life in the city.

But they soon developed ways to catch their fun and invoke the wrath of the left-handed Irish Priest. They organised and attended "discos" and devised ways of evading inexistent and porous security in their hostel accommodation to attend parties in nearby secondary schools and even private parties on Saturday nights. The morning after, they showed up as dutiful soldiers in double files as they made their way, either to the Baptist or Catholic Church.

While I attended Ovu Grammar School from home as a day student, I was privileged to live with my mother in her early years of widowhood. This was probably destiny's way of giving me another opportunity to live with her. I had been temporarily separated from her for a period of five years, when my father sent me off to live with my older sister in a neighbouring city, where I attended an Anglican primary school.

I watched my mother rise as early as 4am in the morning to go to the farmland. She returned to cook us breakfast and the rice she hawked around the village. She also sold provisions during breaks to the Ovu Grammar School students, and that was not all. She secured a contract with the principal to supply fruits to the boarding students. From her I learnt generosity of heart as a virtue. She gave clothes and food items to those who couldn't afford to pay for them. She was industrious, entrepreneurial and was already practising multitasking even before the invention of the word itself. She prioritised people over profit, an attribute which I gradually internalised and was later to be an indispensable part of me. Retrospectively, the only thing I couldn't learn from her was her entrepreneurial spirit and skills, which I suppose, I wasn't wired to acquire.

While I learnt a lot from my father's silence and unspoken words, I learnt from my mother's presence, examples, and words, which she never failed to use to constantly remind me of whose daughter I was. She made his absence feel like he never left in the flesh. I still live with this overarching aura of my father, who I believe, from the world beyond continues to guide, inspire, and protect me in life's journey, personal choices, and lifestyle.

Very early in life, I learnt to have a mind of my own. I've also learnt to be very reflective and inquisitive. I tried to understand reality and the reasons behind the way people behaved the way they did, and the choices they made. I was particularly fascinated by people's ability or incapacity to make rational, conscious, and informed choices. I had seen my father often lost in thoughts, trying to figure things out and use his mental abilities to solve problems. From him, I must have inherited the ability to prioritise thinking over speaking, thoughts over words, and meditation over verbalisation.

Although he had many books as a teacher, I clearly remember only two of them: The Bible and the Missal. He was a very knowledgeable and wise person. Most came from natural wisdom and the application of reason, reflection, and meditation.

With an inquisitive mind, I was a child born outside of my time. I sought understanding and justification at a time I was only expected to accept without questioning. Nevertheless, my mother seemed to have been above the tides of time as well. I often asked her questions and sought clarifications.

"You ask too many questions", she often told me. Sometimes she just repeated the same question I had asked her, using the same words, but ended with a smile. When she did this, I understood there was no answer to my question, or I shouldn't have asked in the first place.

One guarded secret between my mother and I was my refusal to be subjected to the practice of female circumcision, now known as female genital mutilation. It was, and still is a cultural practice. It was part of the rites of initiation to womanhood. It was also part of the initial preparations for marriage. Girls were expected to prove their readiness to enter womanhood, a precursor to the paroxysms of childbirth. I did have my way in evading the imposition of this practice. It was the first battle I won in life, but not without a fight or flight. I had imagined the physical pain it was going to cause me. I was not wired for that, and my mother understood. To be fair, I think it was rather her who won the battle of understanding her daughter and protecting her from the expectations of a cultural practice of violence. She understood me, protected me and stood by me. She had to pay a fine for my sin of omission. From my part, it was a question of defying a practice that made no sense to me, secretly fuelled by my fear of pain, and justified by my instrumentalisation of reason.

I felt I was different as I grew up, although I had no problem with this. I stood against everything girls of my age stood for. I couldn't understand the fun they derived from the things they did: dressing up, crashing parties, drinking alcohol, smoking, or having a regular boyfriend and an occasional "sugar daddy". While some girls thrived on trade by barter, I engaged my mind with the battle of Adam Smith's theory of opportunity cost. I truly believed that in life there was always an important commodity that would be left unbought. My peers believed the contrary. They bought everything they wanted; the end justified the means. I sometimes just stopped at analysing how the means could be justified by the end. Oftentimes, it didn't go further than that.

Because I'm this way, I tend to be extremely sensitive to the exploitation and injustice suffered by others. I don't subscribe to people who use their privileges and positions of honour to oppress others. Given my Mother Theresa syndrome, (coincidentally, my own mother is Theresa), it didn't come as a surprise to me that I decided to become a nun when I completed my secondary education.

Was this a rational and informed decision?

Retrospectively, I wouldn't tell. At that time, it felt like the right way to go, and the only thing to do. Becoming a nun was my first choice in life. My natural inclination was service to humanity. Becoming a nun seemed to be the climax of a destiny already initiated in the secrets of my being.

Was it really a choice?

There was no simple and direct answer to this question. Then it was a choice. Then it was the right choice to make. But decades on, the answer too may have changed, like every other thing that is permanently in a state of flux.

At eighteen, I thought I knew exactly what I wanted to do and where I wanted to be for the rest of my life. How wrong I was. I thought I had figured it out, I felt I could change the whole world. I only realised a few decades after that the world doesn't change. The only way I can change the world is being me in a becoming world.

In my time and as a young growing girl, there were only two options available to me after secondary school. I either got married or became a nun. Even the latter was not a very common and desirable choice. It didn't appear to be the first choice even for those who made that choice at a very early stage in life. It was often considered an option for women who found it difficult to attract suitors because of their looks or for girls who weren't that smart or bright academically.

But there I was. A contradiction of this description. I had a swarm of suitors and very good academic grades that could open the doors I wanted. Yet I opted for what was least expected of me.

Essentially, I was already at an advantage going to school at the time. After completing secondary school, it was the most natural thing that my female peers dreamt and hoped to secure a future of togetherness in eternal marital bliss with their boyfriends, often their first love. Here again, I was the odd one out. I had no declared or imagined boyfriend, although a multitude were ascribed to me and a further legion of men claimed exclusive ownership of me. I didn't lack attention from the opposite sex, but because I was convinced of my choice. It was not an alternative but my only choice at the time. My unavailability made me a greater prey. Early enough I was exposed to the games men played as predators. The more a girl turned them down the more they persisted, often just to prove a point.

A third way between the choices of marriage and the religious life was unthinkably unsustainable. It was already senseless enough to become a nun. This is understandably so for men who justify their vocation with the service of God through humanity. It was absurd for women to follow suit, especially as they do not carry out the same religious functions as men, who for example become priests and say mass as well as administer other sacraments. The job description of the religious woman was not as clearly delineated. It just didn't add up that a young girl in her right-thinking mind would dare to be different, in a cultural environment where opting out was an exception to the rule of blending in at every cost.

I didn't have the luxury to ever consider remaining single, carve out a career for myself, and make lifestyle choices that aligned with my individuality. At that time, a young woman was not expected to 'decide' or choose to remain single even if she were insane. Marriage was the ultimate dream for every young woman, especially of African descent. She was expected to settle down with a man who would take care of her and her family for the rest of their lives. Marriage was and to some extent still is for financial viability and social security. Women were not socialised to be independent, especially financially. But the truth is that life happens and often throws a much more dreaded reality than the one desired.

Many women have woken up to the inevitability of having to be independent at a time least expected; When they have not acquired the necessary skills through formal and informal education; when they have far greater responsibilities; with a litany of children and mouths to feed that would make it impossible for them to take full responsibility of their situation, without considering the only option they know – getting married to another man who would take over from where the previous husband, dead or living dead stopped.

Essentially, a middle-way choice was inconceivable. There wasn't the option to try before you buy. The prevailing culture wouldn't forgive me if I adopted a tried and tested approach to ascertain whether my choice was the right one. If it wasn't right, I could have the option of a U-turn and go the opposite way with absolute certainty. Worse still, there was no return policy. Once married, the next logical stage was to start bearing children. The conscious choice of refraining from having children is inconceivable. The story does not end here. The great expectation for a male child continued for female-only bearing women.

My initial senseless choice didn't need any convincing. I didn't need to try and test the waters. I was absolutely sure. I thought I was.

I fondly remember my decade-long stopover at the convent. I closed the doors to the world and all it had to offer me at the age of eighteen. This was the time my peers opened the same doors to explore the world and simply soaked in all that it had to offer. When I finally closed the doors of the convent behind me at the age of twenty-eight, it was not because I had missed anything about the world I left at eighteen. In all honesty, it was more difficult to return to it than to turn my back on it in the first instance. When I went in, I was celebrated as a heroin. The entire village organised a reception to welcome me back home in the village town hall. My former Principal, the Irish priest couldn't be more delighted of the student who gave him so much headache but then was the only one who took this unexpected route. My mother was ecstatic as she joined the prestigious league of "mama sister". My journey out felt different. I was in Rome at that time and my only concern was how my mother felt about my decision. Contrarily, it was her turn to make me proud. She told me she didn't mind whatever I decide to be in life as long as I was happy with it.

"I'll invite you for her marriage!"

This was her response to a Christian mother who tried to make her feel her daughter was a disappointment. My mother, more than anyone else backed me up, like she always did. She didn't need to judge my choices. She accepted my decisions. This was a precious lesson that I learnt from her and subsequently applied in my relationship with my own children.

My years within the convent confirmed a continuation of my personality. These years consolidated the life of discipline and routine I was already very familiar with. Additionally, they instilled commitment, devotion, detachment, singleness of purpose, dependence on divine providence, structured prayer life, silence, meditation, imitation of the saints, being alone with God and self-solitude as spiritual values and virtues. These have contributed to unfolding and shaping the person that I was and still am today. Essentially.

These years were the most important and impactful in my life. I strongly believe that I wouldn't be the same without them and the experiences of growth and maturity they offered me. They were meant to be an essential part of my journey but not my destination.

I didn't take the decision to leave the consecrated life light-heartedly. I had to go through a year-long spiritual direction with a Jesuit priest, culminating in a three-day retreat where I sought the will of God, spiritual guidance, and discernment. Those three days in isolation, more than anything else confirmed that the decision I was about to take was the right one. It was not about leaving because the lifestyle was difficult to embrace. It was, essentially about a hunger that remained unsatisfied. I felt like I was in the midst of plenty but was still hungry. I was in search of the face of God and didn't find him where I thought he lived, or better still, where I imagined

I would find him. That I didn't find him there didn't mean he wasn't there. This was enough for me to leave, even without knowing where to go next. One thing I was sure I needed to do, and I sure did. I organised a mass of thanksgiving and invited my friends, who were mainly priests and religious. It felt more like the last supper, where Jesus alone knew that his death was imminent. At that mass, I alone knew that the end was close at hand. For me then, it was a *Te Deum* time.

When people leave the religious life as I did, they are judged, condemned, and categorised as backsliders. It's very easy for people to assume that the reason behind is associated with the love of a man or woman. This is precisely what they gave up in the first place. It is what people assume they need and miss most. I think this is a superficial conclusion and this isn't the only wrong judgement hurriedly delivered in their disfavour. They are equally seen as those who have been unfortunate enough to have fallen from the bandwagon, from grace to grass. Contrarily, I feel each case has its individual merit and should be considered as such, rather than adopting a position of syllogistic generalisation. I don't consider myself or any other person in my same situation as a sheep that has strayed from the fold, but as one, who is constantly in search of that one-fold whose chief shepherd is the Lord himself. The religious life is a perfect expression of the way to the Master when all the stipulated conditions are met. It's an ideal way of life that has different implications when applied to reality as it continues to evolve, in a world of constant change, like every human representativeness and activity.

Essentially, I believe that three indispensable ingredients must come together for a choice of this way of life to be legitimated. These are time, place, and circumstance. Time is the most determining factor of the three. We live with the assumption that we have time. We understand time as a concept. We measure time, we even trade time in exchange for money, where people, for the same amount of time, earn differently depending on their skills, jobs, experiences, and positions. We even plan and save for years of retirement, and nurture dreams of a lifetime of the things we would do once the demand of a nine-to-five job gets out of the way. With time on our hands, we fall in love and get married believing it will be forever, for eternity. But eternity is now, no more no less. It is this very moment. We don't know and can't tell if we'd have the next second, hour, or year.

To make a decision based on time which we are not in control of is already in itself flawed. This is the reason time alone validates our previous decisions and confirms whether they are the right or wrong ones. Many decisions we previously made were later revealed to be the wrong or even bad choices, with time. Looking back now, if I had the chance to go back in time, I would, most probably take that same direction, and, most probably again discontinue as I did long ago.

The other two factors I mentioned above are place and circumstance. In my situation, Rome was the place and the context that gave me an enabling environment to take this vital decision. Maybe, if I had been in Nigeria at the time, I would probably not have left. The prevailing culture would have forced me to reconsider my decision and remain for convenience and the fear of stigmatisation.

5

The Roman Factor

Rome for me was both the deal maker and breaker. It gave me exposure and pulled down the walls of protection that the convent, from the African perspective, had, before then, given me. In Rome, I wasn't totally excluded from the world I was running away from. On the contrary, I was fully immersed in it, taking the same public buses while struggling internally to maintain my otherworldliness. Rome was and still is a marketplace, a battleground to fight the good, the bad, and the ugly. For me, it was an arena, a place where many fought to find and retain the faith they brought with them. It was also the place where many lost their battles of faith with fate.

It was in Rome that I made a double leap of faith, which, in all honesty, I can't attribute either to faith or to reason. All I felt then was that I absolutely wanted out. All I had was the strong conviction that I no longer belonged where I initially thought I would be for the rest of my life. Was that a leap of faith? The truth is that God then, was not at the forefront of my decision. He was definitely and secretly in the background, even without my acknowledging it then.

I went to Rome, in my early twenties, armed with the misconception and misunderstanding of the eternal city as the "City of God". I soon faced the reality that it was also a city where men were, where the love of God prevailed over the sin of man. I soon realised the peculiarity of this city of two states, a personification of the perfect and pacific co-existence of the sacred and the profane.

The language, food, culture, and people were different. Even the same Catholic religion appeared to be different at that time, in this part of the world. I could hardly differentiate between their culture, religion, and traditions as they were all interwoven as one single reality.

In Rome, I made my first baby steps in understanding of the concept of reason as a human faculty and how it could be used even in proving the existence of God. I studied logic, syllogism and all the paraphernalia and mumbo jumbos that seemed to make no sense outside the walls of philosophical investigations. I studied under Jesuit thinkers and philosophers. I devoured the volumes of Fredrick Copleston's History of Philosophy and my interest in exploring how far I could go with reason began. I was not only enticed by the world of reason and the miracles it could accomplish, I also became so fascinated that it was later to define, explain, justify, or even contradict and question what I had believed and held true until then, including the way of life I had chosen and had believed to be the permanent choice.

In Rome, I was part of the initial discussion on the existence of African Philosophy. I became exposed to the concept of African Traditional Religion, of the concept of the African God, who is not totally other, distant, transcendent, but one who sits and dines with his own. I engaged with the African concepts of life and death as conditions of the here and now, rather than the there and after. Studying those concepts, some of which I struggled to understand and accept, gave me a sense of pride in being African. I started to embrace my identity and difference in a cultural environment that was openly racist and homophobic by default and design.

In Rome, I learnt the importance of traditions, both in the Church and the family. Catholicism in Rome was more of a cultural and less of a religious practice, especially for young parents, who took their children to Sunday masses in preparation for the sacraments, the same way they would accompany them for other extra curricula activities, like swimming, football, and karate. This wasn't different for me either. I attended Sunday masses religiously and rigorously. This had no impact on my weekly activities or personal life until I returned to Church the next Sunday to fulfil all righteousness. This was also to set the children on the straight and narrow before they eventually made their own choices come age eighteen.

In Rome, I was a professional Catholic, my personal relationship with God then was yet to gradually unfold many years later. This was when experiences in life inevitably led me to make a qualitative leap from a rational to a relational faith in God.

Natale con i tuoi, pasqua con chi vuoi.

These words in a nutshell expressed the importance of the tradition of families, spending Christmas time together, as a non-negotiable norm. Tradition also meant that the family Christmas tree remained the same, year in, year out. The same held for the annual New Year's Eve speech of the *presidente della repubblica* or the recitation of the *Te Deum* on the same New Year's Eve, when people ate *lenticchie*. Eating *lenticchie* once a year created a sense of expectation. It was available all year, but its special role associated with the last meal of the year made it extremely important. This helped me also in building structure, routine, and discipline. It also taught me resilience, to wait and not give in to instant gratification.

Italian women have the practice of fasting, or more appropriately, dieting before every major festivity that would involve a lot of eating and drinking, such as Christmas, Easter, birthdays, and weddings. On average, women lost 3kgs or more each time before the great feasts began. I suppose this was their own way of dealing with the guilt of overindulging. It made sense that they practiced self-denial before gratification, in a way that struck a balance. They created space and got rid of excess fats before they introduced more calories into their bodies.

One very important tradition I learnt was that on the same New Year's Eve, at about midnight, whatever was not needed for the New Year was thrown out of the window in some sort of ritual. It was a dangerous practice as it was possible for old television sets to be thrown out without due consideration for whom it might hit on its way down.

In Rome I learnt healthy eating and how to constantly put a check on my weight. This was not a choice based on health promotion but for a more functional reason. Plus-dress sizes were very expensive and plus sized women could only afford a couple of dresses. Entering an Italian clothing store with a size 44 to 46 was often met with a frown and automatic response of either the shop owner or shop assistant.

Questo non e' per te – This is not for you.

This was just as far as their knowledge and understanding carried them. I already had a 42-shoe size, when Italian women sizes were in the average of 38. I struggled to find my shoe size but more importantly, I learnt not to have too many shoes, a habit I have maintained to date.

I wouldn't be the mother that I am today without the Italian factor as a major influence. I learnt how to be not just a mother, but a good mother from Italy. A mother that didn't put her career first, but built her life around her children; a mother that is a constant presence in the lives of her children, a mother who is there in the morning to see her children off to school, then comes back home to complete all domestic chores, then prepares lunch and then rushes back to the school to pick them up and after lunch and a short rest, takes them for one activity or the other. Most essentially, she is there to help her children in completing their homework. This continues until the child is fifteen or even more. In my experience as an Italian- influenced mother, I embraced my responsibilities and never delegated any. If I had my children somewhere else, this may have been different, but I have not lived to regret my style of motherhood, even when things spiralled out of control, while I was watching.

Italy gave me the opportunity to maintain my paternal roots. It's one of the few countries where it is the norm, not the exception for women to retain their surname at birth and add any spousal surname as suffix. This is one tradition I really cherished and could be the answer to many issues surrounding the preference for a male over female children in most African countries. This way, women's origin is not forgotten or traded off at marriage.

Growing up, I remember columns of some Nigerian newspapers tagged "change of name". This was usually populated by young women: "I, formally known and addressed as.... now wish to be known and addressed as...". They took on both a new title and a new surname in one go. I must say I enjoyed retaining and using my maiden surname in Italy as that was my true identity. When I proudly returned to using my maiden surname after legal separation, a colleague saw me and said "congratulations, I didn't know you just got married".

In Rome, I initiated my first fight for women's liberation. Soon after obtaining my doctorate, I became part of the first African migrant women group, represented at the Beijing conference of 1995, which gave rise to the Beijing

Platform for Action. This was a landmark blueprint for securing equality for women across the world. I was vice president of the *donne intelettuale africane,* founded by Elisa Kadigia Bove, wife of Achille Occhetto, first Leader of the Italian Democratic Party of the Left. With Kadigia, I started my first public discourses and debates on the role and identity of African women. Kadigia and I embarked on a journey of educating the Italian public and significantly distanced ourselves from the then existing model of women liberation, based on the war of the sexes. "Men" were perceived as the common enemy of women, and therefore the proposal of liberating women from male oppression and domination. We, on the other hand, proposed a paradigm shift from the freedom of women from men to a discourse on the freedom of African women from the grips of underdevelopment, their one true enemy. We focused our attention on the complementarity model as the only one applicable to the experience of African women.

My public engagements took me to schools, national and international conferences, Italian television and even brought me to the inner rooms of the Roman Capitol, the seat of the local government administration in Rome. Then, pregnant with my first son, I attended long meetings and debates on the political involvement of migrants at the local government level as a concrete step towards their integration.

Retrospectively, I never enjoyed those meetings. I felt I didn't belong there, despite the potential it offered me to gradually emerge as a public political figure. It wasn't for me. I was looking for solutions and didn't want to be part of the problem. I still had battles to fight, but not from a political platform. Fast forward, more than a decade after our initial battle in the Capitol, the first African Councillor was appointed. He was elected in a parallel voting arrangement where only migrants were allowed to vote for their candidate in a makeshift election – it was a political project that subsequently died and never resurrected.

In Rome, my passion for fighting human trafficking for sexual exploitation took root and started consolidating what was already innate in me. A fire that was ignited while I studied philosophy burnt even more when I came face to face with the contradictions of life as well as social injustice, inequities, and inequalities. My quest all along was the search for an alternative to improve the human condition, through my individual contribution. It was a discomfiting experience to see young girls who ended up on the streets of Italy, when their families believed they had travelled abroad in search of a better life.

In my counter-trafficking activities, I prioritised raising awareness on the education of the girl child, using my privileges and personal testimonial of a father, who many decades ago, didn't have to make a choice of not sending his female children to school. If my father with six girls didn't have the excuse of not sending his girls to school, I think no father should. I believe it is sheer greed to throw them out there and leave their fate with the caprices of traffickers and smugglers, all in the name of a better life abroad.

6

Life at Second Chance

Life has given me a second chance as well as a second choice; more of a chance to make choices. If there was anything that has worked well for me, it was my ability to pick up the pieces and start all over again, without regrets and without being remorseful.

My children are the most precious gift of God to me. It is not coincidental that both gifts were given to me in Rome. I had previously made a secret vow to God when I entered the religious life. On the night of my first profession, I asked God to give all the children he meant for me to one of my sisters who was struggling with a childless marriage. When I finally left the convent, God didn't remind or punish me for my unfulfilled vows to him. He gave children to my sister without denying me of motherhood as I had prayed.

Thank God for unanswered prayers.

Becoming a mother was one of the first concrete signs to me, that God's ways are not ours and indeed, his thoughts are not our thoughts. Maybe my African god would have answered my prayers exactly the way I had wanted them answered and left me to deal with the consequences of my desires. But God could not be limited by his boundless resources. I truly believed the psalmist when he says, "In his register of people he writes, these will be her children" (Ps 87:6-7).

I see being a mother as a vocation, an extension of the sisterhood and undoubtedly a concrete expression of religious motherhood.

Did God give me boys because one of my kind is more than enough for this world? I believe this was another chance He gave me to experience life more intensely from a completely different platform and perspective. If he had given me girls, I would have had to live the same life twice. Raising up boys gave me the chance as well as the challenge to live a different life. With my boys, I kicked the ball, watched male-inspired Japanese cartoons, and laughed without understanding what it was all about. With them I drove toy cars and trains and struggled to knot their ties, the only thing I have not been able to master. It would almost have been impossible if I had girls. Being a mother to boys who later grew into men was a unique opportunity. It was a special calling and a privilege to transform the world through the values I transmitted to them; to enable them to be the persons they would be – kind, humble, simple, respectful and generous, then as men, recognise their harmonious role in the society without allowing themselves to be tagged or defined by societal contradictions and expectations.

If I have had any fear of judgement in the past, it was the fear of being judged as a mother and not as a wife. Even on the last day of judgement, I believe that God would be more interested in how faithful I have been in my maternal duties than in my marital expectations.

As a mother, I am a co-creator with God, and I contribute to making the world a better place through the values I transmit to my children.

As a wife, I didn't even stand the chance of making one man a better person. I stood the better chance of making myself a worse person and I couldn't live with that.

Reflecting on the final judgement and my own individual responsibilities in this world, I recall that when people exchange marital vows at their weddings, it ends with "till death do us part". I would have been more concerned if marriage were a condition for admittance to heaven. Then again, I'm reminded of the interesting passage in John chapter 4. It was the longest discourse Jesus ever had with an individual, and guess what? It was with a woman, the woman at the well. Jesus asked her to go and call her husband and she said "I have no husband" and Jesus said "you are right to say "I have no husband", for although you have had five, the one you have now is not your husband" (Jn 4:18).

7

Life in a Single Dose

One single factor that persistently defined Italy was the lack of employment opportunities. This affected more women and migrants as the number of people migrating to Italy increased year after year. Working Italians navigated between *un posto fisso* and *precarieta*. Permanent working positions in public services or offices were the ultimate dream. This was impossible for most Italians and an absolute off-limits for migrants. There were just some Italian jobs that foreigners dared not aspire to, including driving public buses or taxis. Migrants had even lesser opportunities in the Italian job market unless they worked for a foreign office or an international organisation or simply took on the jobs that Italians themselves wouldn't do.

I was fortunate enough to engage with freelance conferences, trainings as well as occasional lectures and summer seminars on African culture, religion, and gender in one of the state universities in Rome. I also wrote and published research papers in designated journals. I did this alongside my role as a full-time mother and didn't have to choose between a career and the call to motherhood.

Nevertheless, I knew this wasn't sustainable in the long run, especially for my growing children. I was concerned about the future of my boys if they remained in Italy. I was a migrant in Italy, having come from another country of origin. I had a different culture, tradition and values that had shaped my personality. This wasn't the same for them. They were born in Rome, their first words were uttered in the Italian language, which was the only one they spoke and understood. The food they knew was *pasta* and the unmissable accompaniment of *parmigiano reggiano*. They attended Italian nursery and primary schools, and followed their culture and traditions, but this was as far as it could get. In Italy, citizenship wasn't automatic by birthright. If they wanted to become Italians, they would need to apply at the age of eighteen and above.

I took the decision to move to the UK deliberately and consciously. I wanted a better place and opportunities for my children.

Again, this was another decision I made in blind faith. The one, however, that I have never regretted, despite the many challenges and the twists and turns that life in the UK took me through.

I soon realised how different the UK was from Italy. This was not just about the weather. I felt the people were very different and shockingly formal to the bone, unlike the informalities in Italy where friendships were easily established as soon as the initial language barrier was outdone. The boys were very quick to change and adapt to the new environment. They had never seen so many blacks in their entire life until our arrival. Contrary to what I had believed, the family that lived together wasn't necessarily the family that was together. Utility bills in separate names were required to validate partnership, marriage, or cohabitation.

Although the move to the UK was primarily for the priority benefit of my children, I was, at the time unaware of what this would cost me. I was totally unprepared and the price I had to pay was the sudden and unannounced death of my eighteen-year-old marriage.

I have always heard people say that "life happens", but I thought I was too predictable, calculated, and totally in control. I could never have imagined in a million years that life would happen to me this way, like everyone else, without giving me some sort of quit notice, well in advance to enable me digest what was to become my new reality, from this day forward. There I was, suddenly alone with two underage boys, a part-time job and all the household bills to be paid.

In the not-too-distant past, I had started life all over again. But this time was different by all standards of judgement. First, unlike the previous decision, this wasn't taken by me. This happened to me. Again, I had two additional mouths to feed. It was not business as usual.

Nevertheless, I had to hold several conversations with myself. I started with a protracted examination of conscience. I was, at the same time, judge, juror, and convict. I felt it wasn't the time for a pity party or a blame game. I turned to Mary in prayer for direction. As a Catholic, I never really had an intimate relationship with Mary until then, but I felt she was the only one as a mother, who could understand my plight. I received the inspiration to apologise to my children for any way I had failed them as a mother. I acted instinctively, without questioning as if someone was guiding my steps and actions. I can't even remember what I told my children when I entered their room, but that apology was the beginning of our healing process together. Rather than focus on what left me, I channelled my energy on who remained with me. I strongly believed that "if they had belonged, they would have stayed with us" (1Jn 2:19).

Sometimes I come across as a very resilient and a strong person considering some of the challenging experiences that I have passed through. I don't understand where it comes from, what makes me strong, or what experiences in the past have taught me to respond to life's circumstances the way I did. I believe that experience is the ultimate test and teacher, but the experience didn't make me strong. It only brought out the inner strength in me, what I already had within, which I never even knew I had until I had to prove it to myself or to others. All I needed was a platform, a single occasion, which life gave me to stand the test.

A few months into my imposed and newfound singleton, I understood that God was, all along working for my good and in my favour. My deepest and most burning desire was to go back to receiving the sacraments, which eighteen years of non-sacramental marriage had denied me of. My new circumstance meant that I could explore the possibility of reconciling myself with the Church. This gave me new hope, perspective, and strength to look towards the future that I have always desired – that of a fully immersed, integrated and practising Roman Catholic, far away from the professional Catholic that I had become.

I can't forget the immense joy and peace of heart, mind, and soul I experienced at my first sacramental confession. This was followed by the sacrament of the Eucharist. The prolonged years of yearning and waiting gave me a different perspective and attitude to receiving the sacraments. Thereafter, I attended the same mass every day when I could, but each time it was different like I was attending for the first time. I recited the *Credo* with more zeal, mindfulness and vivid faith, every word struck me and sometimes, made a completely different meaning like I was hearing it for the first time. It was the completion of a circle. I felt like the Israelites, at peace and at rest from all enemies far and near. I felt a true sense of belonging to the Catholic Church, once again. I was no longer ostracised or stigmatised for not being old enough to receive first Holy Communion as one of my children asked me at a very tender age. I believe my perception of what people thought about me was all in my mind. Nevertheless, I found a new zeal for attending masses and eagerly looked forward to receiving Christ in the Eucharist, an encounter I never took for granted and for which I was appropriately prepared each and every time.

It was not before long that the enemy struck again in a manner I could never ever have imagined even if I have had ten lives to make a guess.

8

The 'First Lady' That Almost Was

There were times, soon after the end of my marriage that I felt I needed to be in a relationship that would end up in marriage. I was later to realise that not all relationships are meant to go in that direction. I believed I was only playing out societal expectations. Women were expected to be coupled in every circumstance, good or bad. The biblical "it is not good for a man to be alone" is easily replaceable with "it is wrong for a woman to be alone". I have been socialised in a culture where men are always excused, and women shamed. I was independent, complete, healed, whole, lacking nothing.

However, an inner voice kept reminding me that I was incomplete, and that my independence had no place in the world as I know it. I wanted at least to prove a point that I wasn't a bad woman who was too good to be abandoned with her children. I felt I was in the garden of Gethsemane. I needed the agony to go away. I desperately wanted the will of God to prevail in my life. I was like the Master himself, who went from his father to seek comfort in his disciples who were too tired to be awake. I was faced with the dilemma of seeking the face of God and the validation of men. I was between the son of man and the sons of men. I seemingly had everything I needed for life and godliness (2 Pet 1:3). Yet the enemy diverted my attention to focus on the one thing that I lacked which defined and qualified my identity according to the standards of the world I desperately fought not to belong to.

I have learnt from several experiences in life and in different stages and seasons of my life that each time I prayed to God, asking him for something to satisfy my desires of the flesh, the enemy had the perfect way of answering that prayer, above and beyond my wildest imagination in a way that seems to come from God himself. Sometimes, I believed the lies of my heart and had been misled by my own desires until terms and conditions began to appear and sow the seed of doubt.

A casual and unarranged meeting in Rome took over my life even without my knowing or desiring it, at least consciously. What started as an innocent friendship and social connection gradually spiralled into what appeared to me at the time as my destiny unfolding. For almost four years, I lived the secret life of a potential first lady in waiting. I was exposed to the privileges of diplomatic immunity while flanking him. I accompanied him while he attended diplomatic engagements with foreign emissaries and specially to signing those 'registers of condolence' at the death of high-ranking political figures in countries all over the world, mainly ex-presidents and prime ministers. I was chauffeured around the eternal city but often reminded and reprimanded for not waiting for the chauffeur to open the door for me.

It was a fairy-tale lifestyle, which every woman, except me would dream to have. It was foreign and *contra naturam* for me. I struggled to fit into the role.

The time, place and circumstance surrounding our meeting all worked in my favour. It was as if my unsaid prayers had been answered with all the boxes properly ticked. Where else could a Catholic to the bone meet the supposedly 'right person', if not in the Vatican itself? It was also the feast of the Epiphany, the 6th of January when God was believed to reveal himself to the gentles through the three wise men from the East. He too was a Catholic more to the flesh than the bone, but his political ambition was absolute priority. Everything else fitted in to serve and feed this ambition. Including me.

The individual in question was more than I bargained for. He was an aspiring presidential candidate in his country. He had everything figured out, including dating, and proposing to a national of the largest country in Africa just to enhance his chances of political success. He was overpowered by the love for power and influence. He lived in Rome while I lived in London – a distance that was enough for me to keep my "state of grace" intact and untarnished.

In May 2013, he invited me to accompany him as his 'spouse' (as the official invitation stated) to meet the then Italian President of the Republic and thereafter to participate in a series of events organised by the African diplomatic missions in Rome to celebrate the 50th anniversary of the foundation of the OAU, now African Union (AU). I was deeply troubled by this invitation and the exposure it would give me. Officially, I wasn't his wife, and I didn't want to appear as a fit-for-purpose female accessory. I already had my own exposure in Rome and an integrity to protect. It was not in my best interest to be seen together with him. I was conscious of this but couldn't share my concern with him. Then I seemed to be under a spell, he was very persuasive as a character. I was also to later find out that he was manipulative and controlling.

I mysteriously missed my flight to Rome on that occasion. It was the first time ever I had missed a flight. It wasn't a good omen, as a series of unexplainable events worked together to impede my boarding that flight. It was a wake-up call for me. It was time to take a deep breath, take a step backward and reflect on the turn my life had taken over the last number of years.

My reflection led me to moments of truth. I gradually began to understand that all his show of affection and attention were ways of controlling me. I realised that he sometimes took pleasure in making me feel like a woman that needed only to be seen and not heard. I had to be a silent witness and listener to his diplomatic conversations with his colleagues. I wasn't expected to speak unless my express contribution to the conversation was solicited. I couldn't believe this was happening to the same me, the person who spoke at international conferences was expected to just dress up, show up, and shut up, with a perfect ever ready smile on my face when required. Time was never a factor he considered, he expected me to play the waiting game most of the time, with no apology for keeping me waiting, endlessly and timelessly.

While I was still floundering in the darkness that had become my light, God showed up to bring me back to my senses.

I understood later that this was why I missed that flight to Rome. If I hadn't missed the flight, I wouldn't have had the time I had to reflect deeply.

Once again, doubt crept in. I had become so familiar with this feeling of uncertainty that often suggested that I was either on the wrong path or that I needed to make a choice. I still had that initial hunger, I still felt like something was missing. I felt I was more than what I had become or was in the process of becoming. That familiar feeling loomed around my spirit; I felt my destiny was more than being tied to one person – to play a supportive role while he fulfilled his maximum potential as a man. My African roots seemed to have taken the better part of me, but it was a battle I was bent not to lose. I'm a non-conformist and have never known myself to live with compromises. My doubt once again led me to a place of discernment where God intended me to focus on his true purpose for me, which was different from the purpose my heart's desire had lied about and camouflaged as the real deal.

9

Fighting Me – Addiction and Disease

For us human beings, overcoming fear and dealing with the weaknesses that stand between us and destiny is decisive. Finding mine was ground-breaking and recognising it was my first step in the right direction of a successful outcome and triumph over self-limitation and limiting beliefs. Dealing with it opened the way to uncovering my purpose and discovering my destiny.

I think that most of the fights I had fought were battles against me, my inner self, and my desires. The greatest of these was a 'potential' addiction to alcohol. Interestingly, I never really enjoyed alcohol consumption. But somehow, it did find a way to become a constant part of my everyday routine and reality.

Years of living in a wine-cultured country like Italy was a contributing factor. While in Italy, I never drank "socially" as I wasn't a partygoer. But I drank at home while completing domestic chores. I suppose that was my way of dealing with the deficit in my domestic affairs. I was used to sayings such as *in vino veritas*. At times, I purposely drained down bottles just to inhibit my expressions and freedom of speech to say things, especially things I would, naturally and soberly be too careful and calculating not to say.

Before I knew it, I was making recourse to alcohol as a panacea, an escape, and a diversion from my relationship woes, especially after moving to the UK. Here both family and spousal life were very different from the more structured life I had in Italy. In Italy too, I took time cleaning the home, cooking, and taking care of the children growing up. In the UK, on the other hand, the boys were almost grown and had their own routine, needing me less and less as a mother. Then the food was also different. People went to the supermarket to buy cooked or almost cooked food, which was different from the situation in Italy. Food preparation and cooking fresh was a non-negotiable duty and responsibility of every family woman.

Nevertheless, since I had reasons to cultivate this soon-to-be dangerous pastime while my relationship lasted, I thought I'd drop the habit as soon as the motivating factor was eliminated. I had never been so wrong.

I suffered from the yo-yo syndrome. I naturally navigated between two extremities – everything or nothing; abundance or total lack. Philosophy had earlier taught me that virtue was to be found in the middle. Regrettably, this was one area of my life where I struggled to strike a balance between these two contrasting overindulgences. I went "dry" for days or even months, only to reward myself by overstepping my limits. To be honest, I never perceived my habit to be dangerous when pushed to its illegitimate boundaries. Somehow, I managed this situation and felt I was in total control. My habit was domestic-bound and limited to weekends and holidays. Like many others, less or no alcohol was often on my new year's resolution list. But why make rules you cannot break? Some resolutions never went beyond February – just in time to celebrate Valentine's Day in my own company.

Timelessly, I had made deliberate efforts to stop. I knew myself too well. I would only be lying to myself if my effort was focused on reducing or limiting my intake. I knew the ideal solution, but it rather scared me.

My mind often played tricks on me, and my heart told me truthful lies – that every person had a vice. I was no exception to this rule. Essentially, this was my only vice. I needed to keep one to feel fully human, fully woman, and fully alive.

Each time I attempted to quit, my son told me to "expect a relapse". That never made sense to me. I was just too predictable. "That will never happen", I told myself, but that "never" was just around the corner, waiting for the appointed time to strike. When that close-to deadly relapse finally happened, at a time and in a place least expected, I felt this was one moment in time too many. A moment that saw a reversal of roles – I became the child to be looked after and protected. My son became the adult. I never wanted to be in that similar situation again in my entire lifetime. The battle line had just been drawn.

For the umpteenth time, I had a conversation with myself. I had to analyse my triggers. I understood that my lack of control of what was unpredictable made me vulnerable. I knew I was on the right track, once I had been through the stages of acceptance and analysis, but this was just the beginning of the end, which was still nowhere in sight.

I wanted a change.

I also knew that my willpower alone had failed me in the past. It sustained me long enough for a while, just to silence the voice of my conscience, only to scream at me from the rooftops "I told you".

This time, I needed to be saved from me. I needed healing and knew exactly where to get it. I believe that God was only waiting for me to acknowledge my hopelessness and total dependence on him to find a lasting solution to what could be a deal breaker in my destiny. I took my first sip of wine in Rome and to complete the circle, I made a trip to Rome for my final sip to date. This was the 31st of December 2019. I knew this time was for real and my healing was complete. I never since then even craved, thought about or desired a drink.

I had a wilderness experience. It was another battle I had to fight against myself. I was yet to recover from my battle with separation and divorce. This time, my affliction was manifested in the form of a rare skin disease. Strangely enough, it was a disease that affected people of 70 years and above, of specific religion, quite different from Christianity, and with a defined lifestyle such as artificial studio sun tanning. I didn't fit into any of these specifications. My skin had the same appearances of an Ebola victim. I neither travelled nor was exposed to an infected person. During the 3 months of my isolation and desperation, while waiting for a diagnosis I had more than enough time to reflect on the true meaning of life, the essence of physical beauty as well as the irrelevance of physical appearance.

I realised that each time I had a battle to fight, I also needed a compelling reason to win. In this case, the only thing that kept me going and gave me the courage and motive to fight for healing was my pending conference in Italy. I was determined never to miss it. I only wanted to be fit enough to travel. Interestingly, my faith was not in the equation at the time. I had more questions than answers. I just wanted to get by each day. I went to Church every day, but this was more of a coping mechanism. The only way of distracting myself from staring at my skin. It literarily fell apart to reveal a different type of existence and reality which was totally strange to me. I didn't recognise myself beyond the coverage my skin gave to my body. I started to accept my new reality the same day I came across a "blue" black woman. She was dressed in all shades of blue to complement her permanently disfigured and wrinkled person. She was in her early thirties.

Wow! 'It could be worse', I told myself.

From this experience I learnt that nothing happened by chance, I believe that I had to go through this specific challenge for a reason, maybe to humble me, teach me a lesson, prepare me for a mission, or even avert a disaster that would have deviated me from the right path, the one meant for me from the beginning. But the outcome revealed that God has always had me covered, even when I didn't realise it.

The providential meeting, I had with that lady, whose skin condition was a thousand times worse than mine, was the beginning of self-acceptance of my individual situation. Just like what happened with my near addiction to alcohol, I knew that acceptance and recognition constituted the first step in the right direction.

The stage of my living with the disease began. I was conscious of what my reality had become, but I didn't allow this to occupy the central part of my life. Practically, I ignored it. My new routine was managing the condition with medication. This was followed by a routine hospital appointment and blood test until the Covid 19 pandemic struck.

I received a series of letters from the health services, after I had been identified as an extremely vulnerable person, who was more likely to die from the disease if infected. It was overwhelming to receive those letters, week after week, as a constant reminder of my crippling susceptibility. Rather than accept this verdict, I decided to investigate what made me vulnerable. I was amazed to find out that it wasn't my "disease" that escalated my vulnerability and justified the myriad of "stay at home" warning letters I received. On the contrary, it was because of the medication used to manage my condition.

My awareness of the implications of what lay before me, brought me to the only place I knew I could find a solution. I had been on steroids for seven years. I didn't know how many more years this was to continue. There was the possibility that it was to go on as long as I lived. I couldn't live with this. I took it to God in prayer and asked him to heal me. I believed my prayer had been answered. I acted in faith, when I visited the hospital and told the doctors that I was healed and wanted to come off the medication. They thought something was the matter with me, as my conviction confused them. The next routine blood test showed that the disease was in "remission". There was no more trace of it in my blood cells. They believed I responded well to over seven years of medication. They seemed to have forgotten that the medication was only to 'manage' the disease and not to restore me to health. But I knew where my healing had come from, and who had interrupted my entire life of possible dependency on steroids.

10

A Trial of Motherhood

As a mother, I have also heard people say that the worst thing that could ever happen is for her to lose a child to the cold hands of death. It is the natural course of life that parents die before their children. Life has shown, time and time again that yes, this may be the rule, but sometimes also the exception. While as mothers and parents we nurture the dream of a meaningful and fruitfully long life for our children, it equally remains a nightmare we all hope never becomes our own reality.

Personally, the greatest test I've ever had as a mother, was my son's car crash that almost claimed his life. Unexplainably, the accident left no visible physical injury on his body.

Coincidentally (providentially, I would say), this took place on the 3rd of February, the 40th death anniversary of my father. I always lived to remember this day as the day my father entered heaven. My son's ordeal has changed all that, and for good.

It was a day that set a series of sequential misfortune and evil news, one worse than the other. It was a perfect re-enactment of the biblical story of Job. First it was the accident, then depression, climaxed by a prison sentence, just few months, when, despite every contrary wind, he had soared like an eagle and bagged a first-class degree.

But the worse was yet to come.

Like yesterday, I still remember the day he brought me his statement of result. He stage-managed everything to make me believe he had failed. I fell for it. I knew his predicted grade, after having monitored his performance meticulously. But unknown to me, he had secretly worked hard to overturn this verdict. He wanted to surprise me and make me a proud mother. He sure did.

"This is for you Mum", he told me, still faking his failure which I believed wholeheartedly. I tried to scan through all the scripts he gave me, looking for confirmation of my fear. On the contrary, he expected me to discover the surprise for myself, but because I wasn't expecting it, I couldn't see it, the eyes of my mind were too blind to see.

"What?"

What followed was about a ten-minute display of madness or temporary insanity. I was so overwhelmed with unspeakable joy. Like the Nigerian that I am, I expressed my excitement in a way that left both boys confused, contrary to the best news I just received.

For his exceptional performance, he was invited to a special dinner with the Vice Chancellor of his university. To my greatest surprise, he didn't honour the invitation. He didn't also attend his graduation ceremony. For him, these were just details he was happy to do without.

The darkest day of my life was the day I received the news of his sentencing, sometime in the middle of the month of August. A few months before then, I had the premonition that a sword shall pierce my soul too (Lk 2:35). This was the same day, a few months earlier that he had surprised me with his new car. It was my birthday. I was proud of him that he made months of sacrifices and worked many extra shifts to afford the car of his dream. Deep within me, I felt he was still not mature enough to drive that kind of car. I worried about the exposure, especially as a young black boy and the negative attention it would attract. This was one of the few instances that he never involved me in his decision. He kept it totally secret from me. He probably knew I wouldn't have approved of his choice He kept it to himself until the deed was done and my opinion rendered totally useless and inconsequential.

It was the same day of the accident that I started to understand my previous premonition, that a sword would pierce my soul too. God had a mysterious way of preparing me for this eventuality. I was on my way from work, when I saw police vehicles in front of me, in my neighbourhood, shortly before I turned into my driveway.

"Accident on this road? God save them".

I never knew I just prayed for my own son.

I returned to the accident scene and recognised my son's car from his car plate number and people asking, "Did anyone survive?"

'A sword will pierce your own soul too' kept running through my mind. I was emotionless, numb, and confused but strangely, composed. This was one of the few times I never cried, even though I wanted to with all the strength and life in me. The tears just didn't flow freely as they would naturally do in circumstances such as this one, right in front of me like a live movie.

To say the crash scene appeared fatal is an understatement. My priority was to set my eyes on my son. I didn't think, even for a moment that anything irreversible had happened to him. I lost my father at the age of 13 on this same 3rd of February 40 years ago. I felt once was more than enough. I strongly believed that I had a saint in heaven to protect my son's untimely departure. I prayed to my own father to return my son to me. I reminded him that he had gone long before now to overturn the outcome of this day. I knew he wouldn't disappoint me. He didn't.

When I finally arrived at the police station, the officers told me they needed to prepare me psychologically to see him. I couldn't understand why, still unbelieving what had happened. But when they brought him in to see me, I understood why I needed to be prepped. He was taken to the hospital for a brain scan and later sectioned. I was told it could last up to six months.

At that moment, I knew I had a mission to accomplish. I had a battle to fight and it wasn't "against human enemies but against the Sovereignties and the Powers who originate the darkness of this world, the spiritual army of evil in the heavens" (Eph 6:12).

I strongly believed then that I was fighting this battle from the point of victory. I was convinced that since my son survived the crash, every other challenge that followed was just to fulfil all righteousness. I believed his life was spared for a purpose and as a mother, it was my duty to help him find that purpose.

To prepare myself for the mission ahead of me, I had to take a very drastic decision. I had to stop visiting him in the hospital. This was emotionally very draining for me. I had to choose my battlefront, which was not the hospital. I also had to give him the option of deciding to collaborate with his medication routine so as to get well and return home, where I would be waiting for him.

As a mother, I never had to take a more difficult decision. I needed to focus all my attention and energy on finding a solution, in the one place, and in the only way I knew I would find it – in and through the faith I had in the one who held the present and future of my son.

On my way from the hospital, I randomly drove into a Catholic Church and found myself kneeling desolately before the mother and child statue of Mary and the child Jesus.

"You see how you are holding your child? I want to hold mine as well, exactly as you are doing now". I wasn't sure if those were words of prayer, a desperate call for help or a declaration of faith. All I knew was that I walked out of that Church, believing I had received an answer.

Two weeks later, my son returned home. The prognosis of six months suddenly turned two weeks. But it was still premature to claim total victory over the enemy. He seemed to have temporarily left us to return at an appointed time. Unknown to me at the time, he was terrified and tormented by the possible outcome of his trial for dangerous driving, which was ongoing as he struggled to complete his undergraduate studies. He did all he could to spare me the heartache of his innermost fears, which soon became our worse reality, with a sentence of three years for dangerous driving.

The sentence was delivered on the 18th of August. A few days before then, precisely on the 15th of August, I attended the mass of the day in celebration of the glorious Assumption of the Blessed Virgin Mary into Heaven. The Vincentian Priest who officiated at the mass focused on the seven sorrows of Mary and kept referencing "A sword shall pierce your own soul too".

I felt a bit uncomfortable and couldn't understand why he was speaking about the sorrows of Mary on the same day the entire Catholic Church celebrated her assumption into heaven, which was a triumph, a moment of victory and not of sorrow.

At that time, in my personal life, I have already had too many sorrows that I needed another type of message, anything but sorrow to lift my spirit. I was soon to realise, barely 48 hours that that message was meant for me. And when this happened, I understood that God was preparing me for this great moment of trial through that indigestible but timely sermon.

Four years before then, I had opted to visit a youth offender's prison in my neighbourhood to celebrate a milestone birthday. I attended mass with more than a dozen of them, mostly blacks. I watched how they were heavily guarded. I fixated my attention on the prison officers and their bunch of uncountable keys. I imagined if

St Peter himself had as many keys to let people into heaven. I guess there were no keys to hell.

The young offenders appeared relaxed to be marshalled in for mass. I believed most of them would rather not be there if they had the choice. But it was a place where they felt truly free, at least for half an hour and it was definitely worth it. It appeared a senseless way for me to mark this occasion. Worse still, it was the most unlikely place people would think of spending time on this unique occasion. Thinking about it, years on, I understood God was working behind the scenes to prepare me for the cup which I must drink without delegating it to someone else.

The next station of my *via crucis* just began. My first reaction to the news of my son's sentencing was an internal struggle with a deep sense of guilt and failure as a mother.

Where did I get it wrong? Was I too present to be this absent? I thought I had done everything as a mother, to have chosen my children and their welfare as my absolute priority above everything else? I thought it was sufficient for me to have built my life and work around them – being there when they woke up in the morning and when they went to bed at the end of the day? What else could I have possibly done that I didn't? I thought I was sowing wheat all along and just couldn't figure out at what time, day, or night, under my watchful eagle eyes of a mother the enemy sneaked in secretly to sow tares.

I survived this period through the power of remembrance and the strength of thanksgiving. I recalled the many times in the Bible that God told the Israelites to remember and never forget what he had done for them in the past. He even instituted feasts such as the Passover to remind them not to forget how he had intervened in their favour in difficult times. I had to remember God's goodness, mercy, and favours in the immediate past. I reminded myself that the worse was behind me. If God had saved his life, the same God would protect this same life that was only temporarily being denied of human freedom.

"At least he is still alive", I consoled myself.

I knew it was a question of time, I needed to give time to time, knowing that in the spirit, my son was free and free indeed.

I cultivated an attitude of gratitude as another phase of my trial of motherhood began. I remember the story of the lepers that were healed by Jesus and how the only one who came back to thank him also received much more than physical healing. Psalm 117 was my favourite psalm at this time – "I shall not die, I shall live and recount the blessings of the Lord. I knew this was going to end someday and that I would use it to testify to God's glory and faithfulness. I started to imagine those 3 long years as the 3 days that Jesus lay in the tomb. The Bible says the earth could not hold him, he must resurrect as it has been written. My son must arise.

My challenge then was to ensure that he didn't become a worse person, that he wouldn't be broken by this terrifying experience, and that the freedom which was taken away from him would be used by God to mold his personality. I specifically prayed for God to use this wilderness experience to let his face shine upon him and be gracious to him.

My acceptance of his sentence as a place of purification and encounter with God changed my perspective. I started imagining him in a boarding school, a place of transformation and refinement. I believed he would come out a totally different person, as if this experience was necessary for him to grow.

Patience, they say, is not just waiting but what you do while you wait. This was also time for me to grow in the Word of God to use it in encouraging him, feed and his spirit so that his body would not give in to his surrounding circumstance.

In my curiosity, I went through sections in the bible where the word "prison" was used and found out, to my greatest excitement that the mission of the Christ also was "to proclaim liberty to the captives (Lk 4:8) or set prisoners free. In Matt. 25:36-37 Jesus said, "I was in prison and you came to see me". A total game changer for me was Matt 5: 25 where Jesus said, "come to terms with your opponent in good time while you are still on your way to court with him, or he may hand you over to the judge and the judge to the officer and you will be thrown into prison". Jesus didn't speak about any category of offense here. I particularly found consolation in the words of the letter to the Hebrews – "Keep in mind those who are in prison, as though you were in prison with them". (Heb13:3).

What I understood was the power of the judge who may not be just in pronouncing judgement. It was all a human process of handing over, just as Jesus himself was handed over in judgement. The bottom line was that there is no justice in the world. If there were, then we wouldn't be praying for God's kingdom to come. The world would have been a perfect place.

While my son was in custody, I met mothers who never wanted to own up or speak up about their children's ordeal with the criminal or social justice system or their children going to prison, for whatever crime they committed. To some extent, I would understand, if such crimes were serious crimes such as murder rape, child abuse and drug trafficking.

Many mothers, whose sons were convicted of similar offences, such as dangerous driving were ashamed of disclosure instead of using their experiences to warn others as a deterrent so that other mothers do not suffer the same fate. But how would things change, if we are busy being too ashamed of what, on the contrary should be shouted at the rooftops?

Young people, mainly male, between the ages of 18 and 25, especially of black origin are extremely vulnerable in the UK. It is their vulnerability that makes them visible and easy targets to discrimination, harassment, arrest or even death. We blame it on racism and witch hunting of the black race, we keep calling on the government to tackle knife crime and other discriminatory practices against our young, male black children who are 5 times more likely to be stopped and searched by the police, more likely to be victims of violence and knife attacks, more likely to be convicted and handed a harsher sentence like my son.

But his sentencing was not the end of our ordeal.

While putting evidence documents to mitigate against his liability to deportation, barely 2 weeks into his sentencing, I came across a newspaper article, where a non-black who killed someone did get away with a more lenient sentencing, totalling less than a dozen months, unlike my son. I also read about another non-black young university girl who attacked her boyfriend, yet the judge didn't send her to prison simply because she was a "potential first-class graduate". My son made first class, not a potential, predicted or possible grade, yet received a harsh sentence than those who also committed murder in the same act of dangerous driving.

Would this have been different if his skin colour were different?

I don't have an answer to this question. The issue of race and racial discrimination is as permanent as poverty itself. It will not go away, even if we all change our colours or become as colourful as the peacock. Or as colourless as water. Then we will be accused of making ourselves "intentionally" too colourful or too colourless. I am sure if we dig deep enough, we will find a piece of legislation that could be used in our condemnation. We can only live with it, address, and redress it.

As a mother, I'm more interested in addressing what makes our children more vulnerable. This includes a re-visitation of our roles as parents and the values we transmit to them, especially material values and the false illusion that they will gain acceptance, recognition and will become equal with those who discriminate against them once they have what "they" have. The irony is that it is the confusion of equating "being" and "having" that makes them even more vulnerable to the criminal justice system.

Yet we continue to wage war against intolerance, discrimination, homophobia and of course racism which goes beyond skin colour to include attitude towards difference and diversity in being, having, thought life, behaviour, lifestyle and even religious beliefs, traditions, and cultures.

11

The Power of Choice

Through my personal experiences, I have understood that the power to choose is a luxury that most people are unable to afford.

"I don't have a choice" is an expression I often hear.

But contrarily, everyone has a choice, the ability to express own preference, alternative or choose between two or more options regarding personal life and other complex choices. Sometimes, when people say they have no choice, it means that they have, in fact chosen, or settled for the easier, less complicated, and more convenient option. Interestingly, some people are simply afraid to make a choice. They push others to decide for them so as not to be responsible or blamed for any future consequence. In such instances when change is the desired goal, many leave this to chance or accident as if life just "happened" to them, when they have the power to actively make choices.

The power of choice is intrinsically linked to freedom. When you have choices, you are also able to select from a list of possible options that will lead you to take a decision. Choice also gives you control, and this is where real power lies.

Unfortunately, we live at a time and in a culture where the power of choice is systematically being taken away from us. Worse still, we relinquish that power to others, to the society, to culture, to tradition, to social media in the same way as Esau, in the Old Testament traded his birth right in exchange for a bowl of porridge. Being different is what makes us unique, but are we really allowed to be ourselves? Can we dare to be different without the fear of standing out in an environment that defines outstanding as being totally compromised in an ethnic salad bowl?

I have made choices, some of which I regret. If I hadn't made those choices and taken those chances, I will never have learnt, grown or even progressed. An Italian friend of mine used to say that it is better to regret doing something than to remain with the guilt of not having tried at all. For most part of my life, I struggled to accept her thought. I totally embraced the Catholic teaching which protected me against avoiding "occasions" for sin. More recently, I have shifted grounds, not by avoiding, those occasions, but by fighting through them, yet emerging victorious after the fight and not simply by taking flight.

Another choice I have made in life is to live a simple, quiet, and private life when a life of complexity and abundance are easier and less complicated options the majority would aspire to achieve. In choosing simplicity, I don't believe that any material accumulation and display of possessions would add or deduct any value from who I am, absolutely. In the same way, I don't think that wearing a glamorous or beautiful dress adds any value to my being. This would be the dress wearing me. On the contrary, I would want to be the one wearing the dress and giving it value and not the other way round. Focusing on the accessories and add-ons in life makes us easily forget the real essence of our being.

I choose contentment and fulfilment. Essentially.

I embrace being a woman, created in God's image and likeness. I didn't want to use the word 'choose' as I really have no option here, though we live in a time where this too, has become a choice. I choose to be a silent witness, like Mary, who pondered all these things in her heart and like the Mary, the sister of Martha who sat at the feet of Jesus, listening to him, rather than busy herself with all the pleasantries and distractions of serving and entertaining friends and guests. Jesus says she has taken the better part, which will not be taken away from her (Lk 10:42).

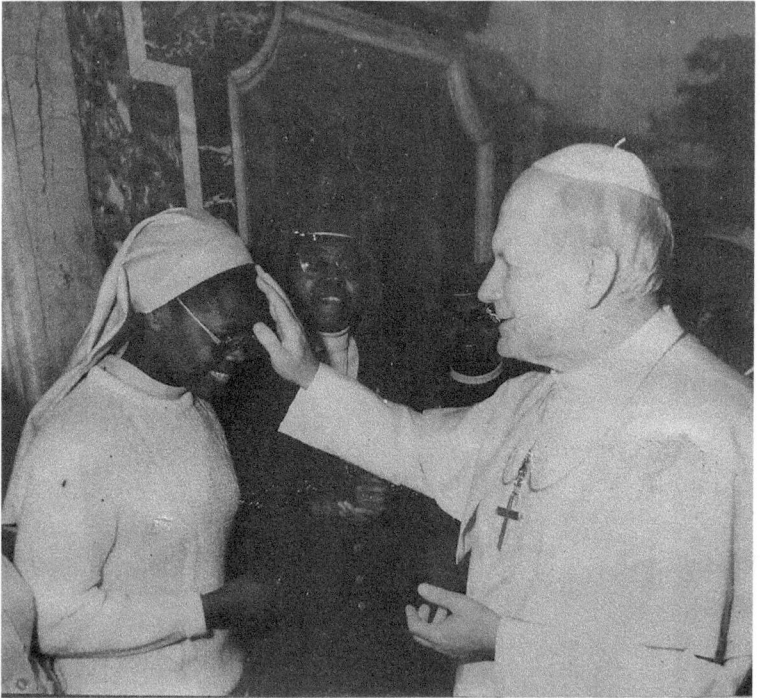

With Pope John Paul II, now Saint Pope John Paul II

12

In the Fullness of Time

Death and the world beyond are hardly part of any healthy conversation. There is a shroud of mystery surrounding death as something to be dreaded, avoided, or if possible mitigated. But death is as real as life itself, different sides of the same coin. The moment a person is born is also the same moment the count-down to the end of life begins. Everything that has a beginning, must also have an end. But death is not the end of life, but the beginning of another type, quality, or category of life.

In life, I've seen how people prepare to meet important personalities, but do not take the time to prepare to meet God himself, the Creator of the universe. Many people pass through life and just allow death to 'happen', uncaring about what happens after life. Many are too busy living the life of their dreams that they forget the inevitable, not the unexpected. Yes, it is true, 'you only live once' and it is equally true that you only die once.

I remember too how I meticulously prepared to meet Pope Saint John Paul II when he visited Nigeria in 1982. It was such an overwhelming and exciting experience with a mixed feeling of anxious anticipation. We waited hours only to catch a flimsy glimpse of his pope mobile as he drove past. I felt the same, when years later, in 1987, I had the opportunity to meet him during one of his masses in his private chapel in the Vatican City in Rome. If I were to have the chance to see him again in the flesh, I am sure the same emotions would accompany my expectation.

This description is the closest I could come to explaining my thirst and hunger to meet and see God, in the fullness of time. Happy are the pure in heart, they shall see God, says Jesus in the beatitudes (Mt 5:8). My hope is that that moment does not find me at the wrong place and time, as I strive to enter through the straight and narrow path of life. I constantly remember the parable of the ten bridesmaids or virgins and do not want to be among the five foolish ones, who ran out of oil and missed the arrival of the groom when they went out to buy some. This parable concludes with the injunction to "stay awake, because you do not know either the day or the hour" (Mt 25:13).

Until the fullness of time, I see myself as the Roman soldier, depicted in Ephesians 6, carrying the shield of faith so that I can use it to put out the burning arrows of the evil one... and the word of God from the Spirit to use as a sword (Eph 6:14-17). I have come to know, understand, and experience God as the One who always operates, not by chance or accident, but by design, purpose, and appropriateness. Ecclesiastes says, "there is a season for everything, a time for every occupation under heaven" (Eccl 3:1).

Until the fullness of time, I am fighting the good fight to the end, I am running the race to the finish, I am keeping the faith as I wait the crown of righteousness which the Lord, the just Judge will give me on that Day (2Tim:4:6).

Until the fullness of time.

In the fullness of time.

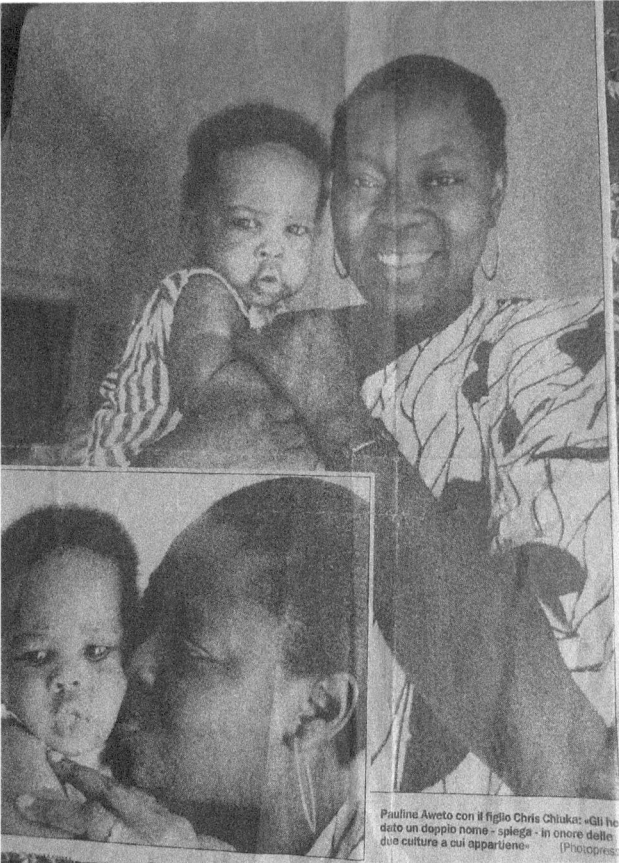

"Pauline Aweto with son Chris-Chuka. I have given him a double name, she explains, to reflect the 2 cultures he belongs to." Published in Roma Cronaca, August 1994. Source Photopress

PART II

THE LINES BETWEEN US: BREAKING THE BARRIER OF STIGMA AND SILENCE

"Nobody in the world could trouble us
Turbulence on our spirit gives us no surprise,
All the blood and the tears of our naked eyes,
The sunshine of our dreams have made them dry"

Chris Chuka Eze Hambrook

13

Letters to My Son

2.09.18

Arise My Son,

We just returned from mass. It's not been the same without you here, but you know you have mostly been absent recently. It was God's own way of preparing us for this new development. I mourned you when you were away with your new family. It is even worse now because I cannot just pick the phone and call you, and hear you say "Mum are you alright? As if I can only call you when things go wrong. Never Mind. I don't miss our Sunday morning quarrels, when I would want you to come to Church. Enough of all of that now. I'm happy I can write as many letters as possible. Expect to receive one each day if possible. I know how bad you feel now, always remember the law of Murphy, things could be worse.

I am trying my best not to preach but you know I can't do without. I am still trying.

On the brighter side, we are all doing fine. Your being away is an exam or a test for all of us. You will come back to us a different person, stronger, bigger, better, best, ready to fly like you always wanted to. You will also meet us better people.

V. is currently studying for a master's degree in the department of PATIENCE. I'm sure she will come out with first class.

Your absence has brought us so close. Last week I fed P. She is growing so fast and not as fussy with eating, unlike you when you were a child. She just ate everything. Definitely she is an improvement of all the *wahala* you gave me as a child.

Hmm I'm just writing. Maybe to fill up the space, but never mind. Royal Mail has to earn the money I pay on postage stamp.

My mum was 87 last week. She did pray for you, for giving her a "white grandchild".

Whatever it is now, I want to assure you that we are all strong and really need you to be. Use this time wisely and profitably. You are a creative artist with first class honours degree. *Haba.* Use this time to write and compose those lyrics that would blow the entire world away. Just WRITE, WRITE, WRITE, even on toilet tissue if there is no paper.

You can also keep a journal, or think of how you can use your experience to impact others. Remember GOD HAS A PURPOSE FOR ALLOWING YOU TO GO THROUGH THIS. HE WRITES STRAIGHT ON CROOKED LINES.

Mark this son, you will be out long before you know it. Can you imagine, it's the 3rd week already?

Take courage, strength from the knowledge that this has an expiration date. Look forward with great expectation to the day you will finally gain your freedom.

What a great day that would be. It will come. I live for this. God bless you son.

Mum

5.09.18

Arise My Son,

I hope this meets you well. We just finished our morning prayers. It is something K. and I started since you left, it reminds me of the waiting for Jesus at Xmas. The waiting may seem long but it will surely come to an end. THIS TOO SHALL PASS AWAY, SEE THE END IN VIEW, FOCUS ON THE DAY YOU WILL EVENTUALLY GAIN YOUR FREEDOM, and think of what you would want to do first.

In the meantime FOCUS, FOCUS, FOCUS, and keep your mind busy. An idle mind they say is the devil's workshop.

I keep myself sometimes listening to music, I wish I have some of yours.

I was eagerly looking forward to seeing you tomorrow, but V. just told me the booking was not confirmed. She said "It made me laugh" Which is a good thing though sarcastic. I told you she is in the department of PATIENCE.

We have no choice but to wait no matter how long we will get to see you.

Meanwhile, this does not stop the passage of time. It goes slowly but the important thing is that it goes, anyhow, anyway.

The next days now are Tuesday 11th and Thursday 13th next week. Hopefully our appointment gets confirmed.

I really wish, hope, pray and trust that you are absolutely fine. Let no one scatter your *DADA*, let no one RUFLE YOUR FEATHERS. Be good and kind all the time, things can't be worse.

I would like to read from you every now and then, it is strange how near, yet how far apart we are.

Remember to turn to God in prayers.

God bless you son.

Mum

10.09.18

Arise My Son,

Greetings, I don't have much to write, knowing I will be seeing you soon. Finally, we can see you this Thursday Morning.

I really want to thank you for making me a proud mother and grandmother. Everything will be just fine.

Mum

17.09.18

Arise My Son,

I know this will meet you well, I am encouraged each time I sit to write to you as I always have a vivid picture of when I visited you. You were strong, courageous, confident and calm. I know the peace of God is with you. I particularly remember you and V. together as you tried to say goodbye to each other. I have never seen that look on your face before. It was a perfect scene of a romantic reality movie. Awesome. As usual, remember to be of good behaviour all the time, remembering your identity and destiny. You are only currently being tested to be trusted, a time to invest in yourself so that you can harvest in due course. Remember the song 'I know who God says I am, what he says I am, where he says I am, I know who I am. I'm working in power, I'm working in miracles, I live a life of favour, I know who I am'.

Peace, Shalom, God bless.

Mum

23.09.18

Arise My Son,

Happy Sunday, I can't imagine where to start. Definitely this would be my last letter/message before I travel tomorrow for my international conference on human trafficking. It's my comfort zone, something I enjoy and could do for free, hope to save souls but the soul I need to save first are those of my family. K. is right, the first reading comes from the book of wisdom. It says "Let me test him with cruelty and with misfortune, and put his endurance to the proof" (WS 2: 12, 17-20) . Does this say anything to you? I don't know what to say right now, sending your letter to the HO to meet the deadline was a real history. Everything worked against it but we thank God it's done.

Mum

01.10.18

Arise My Son,

I had already written a very long letter which I wanted to post on Thursday morning but other thoughts came to my mind during the night especially after reading some articles about the deportation of EU citizens. Your case is not unique, I just want you to be strong, do not blame yourself and remember that life has no rewind button, just press play. I know I supported your decision but we still have a last card to play. You have not officially been served with the "Intent to deportation notice" Once you have this you have 2 weeks to respond. I am going to speak to immigration lawyers today, for a legal representation of your case before the final deportation decision, if it comes to that. What we will not do is appeal the decision. For now this final decision has not been taken so let's not give up hope yet. Remember, your letter to them was "Personal" and not "Legal". So please, call me immediately when you receive the formal notice in writing giving you two weeks, so that we can get to reply within the time frame. I will ask as many questions as possible. In any case, God is in control of everything and I believe things will work in our favour. I have to post this letter now. I might write another one today or tomorrow giving you details of what I find from the lawyers. Remember to call me as soon as you receive any notice. Always be of good behaviour, we are all happy about how positive you feel despite the odds. Do not feel condemned by the present, just focus on what lies in the future. God is with you and He will give you strength to go through this, He is indeed your strength and your shield.

God bless you son.

Mum

3.10.18

Arise My Son,

Greetings in the name of our Lord, I'm sure this meets you well. I sent you a letter on Monday barely 2 days ago. From the look of things they may come together.

Mum

08.10.18

Arise My Son,

Yes, it's Monday and I just returned from Mass. I hope this meets you well. Be very strong because you have support from your family and friends. Just look beyond the here and now. We are doing fine. I have so many ideas which we will discuss on Thursday. You know things could be worse, for example, I will be attending the funeral of that young child on my birthday, the 19th. What do I tell her mother? I am a million times better, you are alive and well. You will only come out bigger, better, and stronger. Son I really want you to be strong, of good behaviour and especially very prayerful. Never mind where you are not. Mind what is in you and where you are going. Because son, you are going places, the enemy can only try but can never stop you. God bless, see you sooner than you expect.

Mum

14.10.18

Happy Sunday My Son,

I remember what you said about Sundays and the calm effect of attending mass. I wanted to be synchronised to your waves. Let's start with this Sunday reading from the book of Wisdom. It starts with "I prayed and understanding was given to me". It goes on to say how precious wisdom is, more than beauty wealth, glory, riches. Wisdom is a gift from God, sometimes taken to be understanding. You can get understanding and knowledge through reading or research. Wisdom is a gift which you cannot achieve through studies. For example my mum is wise, she is not even educated. Wisdom gives you the ability to choose between wrong and right. What about the gospel reading? Christ told the young man who wanted to know what to do to inherit eternal life "There is one thing you lack" "Go, sell all your belongings, give the money to the poor and come, follow me". Wow! You didn't have to come to this, but your situation is similar. Your sentence has stripped you of everything, yet you are stronger than ever. Now you know what matters. It has been a good day, K. and

I went for the 8am mass in St Paul's. I still intend to do the thanks giving, your first class honours, P.'s baptism and your release, yes, your release. Can you imagine all of us in one house? I met O. that guy from Italy whom we met while in Goldcrest. He came for the 8am mass on his way from work. He says HO losses 90% of their cases because they have not even read them. He also thinks you were not properly represented but that is history. By the way, I also went for a programme yesterday organised by the university of G. on diversity. I don't want to bore you with details. Hopefully you would have had a better picture after your EU lawyer has seen you. Did you notice I'm writing in green? Will explain. After you must have gone through all this, I really wish you become a youth ambassador to speak in Churches so that what happened to you will not happen to anyone else.

Mum

18.10.18

My Dearest Son,

Words are not enough to express the immensity of joy I feel today. Words fail me. It has become a routine for me to check the post daily. Often I came back disappointed, as no message from you often meant the end of the day for me. 11am today was different. I opened the mail box and saw 2 letters from you. One was my birthday card/cards. I am still speechless, you have always been a last minute person but this time you beat yourself to it. They arrived not "on time" but "in time". Strangely enough I consider this to be my best birthday ever, you have given me more than enough joy even from a distance. Where did you get the idea of sending me a card as a dad? I so much have the lyrics and have not stopped crying – "Nobody in the world could trouble us" "Turbulence on our spirit gives us no surprise, all the blood and the tears of our naked eyes, the sunshine of our dreams have made them dry" Wow! Thank you so much son.

Another interesting part of the day, V. came to see me with my beautiful and gorgeous granddaughter. It could not have been a better day. As a child you frown or spat out the food you didn't like. She walloped all the jollof rice after the initial *disgusto,* that reminded me of how you refused to eat the food in the village that your paternal grand mum prepared for you. I still have the photo, P. is your refined version and I love everything about her. She has a rare feature, she has gap or what we call "open teeth" It's so beautiful when she smiles. Some African men specifically ask for women with open teeth and are ready to pay anything, I think this just came natural to her as nobody, I mean nobody in our family or even V's has this unique feature. V. told me how people stop her on the street because of her.

Chances are we might not see you next week, but remember turbulence on our spirit gives us no surprise. I had a lot to share with V. today, we both laughed when I told her how your aunty F. expected her Persian cat to chase mice! It was not in its nature, it was not created for this. It was meant to decorate the palaces of princes and royals. ALWAYS RECOGNISE WHERE YOU TRULY BELONG, IN SPITE OF PREVAILING CIRCUMSTANCES. Remember the story I told you about the eagle who grew up amongst chickens? Use this time to flap your wings, because when you finally take off, no one can stop you not even yourself, "We will fly into paradise, success the only one thing on our minds". By the time you read this I must have heard from your lawyer and her visit to you. Please from now on, tell any immigration officer that visits to speak to your lawyer or that your lawyer is handling it.

I cleared your room today and Victoria was surprised at the space. Your things are all intact because I know you will return here sooner than later. I will be spending tomorrow, the 19th at the funeral of the 7-year-old I told you about. As a mother, I'm better off, other people's challenges make you know and appreciate our challenges. Thanks again son, for making this my happiest birthday, your absence makes all the difference and even the more special. God bless you son.

Mum

25.10.18

My Dearest Son,

Finally, "This is what I pray, kneeling before the father from whom every family whether spiritual or natural, takes its name. Out of his infinite glory, may he give you the power through his spirit for your hidden self to grow strong, so that Christ may live in your heart through faith, and then planted in love and built on love, you will with all the saints have the strength to grasp the breath and the length, the height and the depth, until knowing the love of Christ, which is beyond all knowledge, you are filled with the utter fullness of God". "Glory to him whose power, working in us can do infinitely more than we can ask or imagine..." (Ephesians 3: 14-21). This is today's first reading, I just started writing it without even meaning to. Finally our first miracle is here. Your transfer to M. is the beginning of many good things to come. All the *wahala* with B. is finally over. Just like that – Can you imagine? V. was so upset when she couldn't book for us to see you today. They just didn't approve the list for no reason. Little did we know that our disappointment was for a better appointment, and the bad news only was an incubation of the good news. It is evidence that our God is able to do much more than we can ask for or imagine. "Just like that", only put your faith in him, I believe that the news of your release will come even more suddenly than expected. God has a purpose and a plan. He is preparing you for the unimaginable. I am happy knowing that you are in a place with better toilets and facilities. I'm sure it's more humane to be in M. Can you imagine, I even called today and I was given the information I needed, rather, then, the 3 hours wait to no avail in B. Yes, we are all fine and should see you next week at 2pm. I have been busy gathering all the evidence, I have put so much together. Son, I hope you are really better now, Now let me shock you "Nur um dem hofungnsloss haben uns hoffnung gegeben" Yes, still remember this in German, 'it is only for those without hope that hope is given to us'. I look forward to hearing from you soon, I'm happy to know the progress you are making with Church related activities, reading in the Church is great, by the way, a person who reads in the Church is called a lector. Just continue to be of good behaviour. I have no doubt in my mind because you have goodness inside of you. Do not allow people define who you are, don't give them that privilege. God bless you richly son, as you strive to discover his purpose.

God bless you son.

Mum

26.10.18

My Dearest Son,

I am so excited to write again, after the letter I sent you yesterday. They may actually come together but that's really no problem. You will find enclosed in this letter, a brochure on prison week which was actually last week. It contains a series of prayers for those in prison, their families and those who work with them. Please read thoroughly. It will help you to understand and cope better. It will also help you to understand the frustrations of those who work with prisoners. Come to think of it they too are prisoners, but on a part time basis. I'm sure they have their challenges too. I have been reading about M. and saw some pictures, both from the external and internal, it's such an old structure, better than B. though. It gives me so much joy that you are in a better environment, I also read that M's prison was built to reflect the normal life of the city so that prisoners live as normal as possible. Is this true? Anyway. There is nothing to lose in just trying. Can you imagine Xmas things are already out in the stores? Sheer madness. I hope we get to visit you on Xmas day, before or shortly after. I am looking forward to seeing you next week. Please make sure you are of good character all the time. A. says much depends on how you behave. Get involved in as many activities as possible. The online masters in psychology would have been a huge success story, at least you don't have to pay for it, then it will show how reintegrated you are after the sentence. You need to do the needful. Remember you will need certificates of completion as evidence. These people feed on evidence. I have spent the last 3 days putting evidence together for your case. I will go to Woolwich to photocopy 32 pages as I am running out of ink. I am only waiting for A's statement before sending the list of evidences required. They should be more than 60 pages excluding the medical reports which she already has. I will go to her office to deliver them as I don't want any *wahala* after so much efforts to put them together. It is already Saturday morning, I've been up since 3am. I just want to post this now, hoping you receive it before we visit your castle on Thursday. Please remember John 1:5 A light shines in the darkness, and the darkness could not over power it.

You are that light, shine on.

Mum

27.10.18

My Dearest Son,

Things in M. have been exceptional, but I hope that you have been able to attend mass today. Let me start by sharing few things about the readings. The first is from Jeremiah 31: 7-9. "They had left in tears, I will comfort them as I lead them back! The responsorial Psalm is Ps 126 and I want you to read the whole of it, I underline the following "When the Lord brought Zion's captives home, at first it seemed like a dream" I look forward to your freedom "Then our mouths filled with laughter and our lips with songs". I look forward with unfailing hope and trust in the Lord that you will come back, safely and sound to us. The gospel is from Mark 5, where Christ healed the blind man, and restored his sight. Many people tried to stop this man from crying out to Jesus but he cried all the louder, Jesus, Son of David, have pity on me. Do not ever let people stop you from where you want to go or who you want to be. When Jesus finally got his attention, he asked "What do you want me to do for you?" Jesus knew he was blind but still did ask him. This means, even if God knows our needs and desires, he still wants us to ask. "Lord that I may see" The blind man said. He didn't say "But you see I'm blind, just let me see again my friend" (Laughing) Wow. I have been having a swell time, since hearing of your transfer to M. It is an indication that things will work in our favour, that God is always on our side. By the way, do you know time is a human condition and that God is timeless? For him 1,000 years are like a day. Can you imagine? God actually thinks you are imprisoned for a few seconds and not the years you imagine. It is good to know how things work in the mind of God, so as not to misunderstand his judgement or even sentence. I am at peace son and so should you. Life is a battle, but this is God's own war, he will fight on our behalf.

Mum

3.11.18

Dear Son,

As you can see I started writing this letter more than a week ago, but just could not complete it. I am writing this now after seeing you on Thursday, I am even more at peace because you are doing well. Just a couple of things, A. needs to speak with you, she wants to know if you have a number or whether she can send you an e-mail. Please contact her. I also wrote to her about your desire to appeal your sentence. She wants to review everything first, meanwhile, I took a copy of Inside Time, a prison newspaper and found it is really useful. Please read it. It also has so many details of solicitors in different fields. God bless you and happy Sunday tomorrow.

Mum

5.11.18

Arise My Son,

I just read all your 4 letters in one. Honestly, since your transfer from B. I have been so peaceful that I no longer check the mail anxiously. Reading from you was a real pleasure. You never know what skills you have until you use them. I'm sure princess V. (by the way I'm still the queen mother) never knew she could be so patient until her patience was tried and tested. I can assure you, she has graduated with flying colours. You mentioned so many things in your letter, some of them have been overtaken as I saw you last week. I'm unable to come in this week, too many engagements including attending mass at 7pm. I'm sure V. will be pleased to have you all to herself without "sharing" and distribution without contribution. The week after, I will come with your brother, but still with V. and P. You must see them every week, no matter what. Your brother, my boy has grown, is growing. I was so impressed. Please remember to pray for the prison officers. The last time we visited you, V. told me she had always seen the prison walls without knowing what it was all about. Sometimes we need to go into other people's world to know how fortunate we are. Those who do meaningful jobs are not rewarded accordingly. It is a shame. I trust you, my son. Like you said in your letter, we have come a long way as a family. I'm happy, it is a moment of great learning. By the way, yesterday I was almost involved in a ghastly accident, right there in Thamesmead. I had gone to pick a friend to drop her off to work. We later found the car was being chased by the police. I just thanked God that he saved me. If they caught up with him, it would still be dangerous driving. If he is a national, he will be fine. Otherwise, if he meets a judge like the one you had, immigration would rear its ugly head. Can you imagine?

Speaking about next week I will be delivering a talk to the Catholic Women Organisation on human trafficking. There is so much to be done. You know what? God is always on our side no matter whatever happens. He will turn our mess into a message and a miracle. As things stand right now, I know you will grow no matter the soil or ground you are planted. V. is a good woman, but as time goes on, when you have made things really clear with her, then you would not need the friendship of people like M. Son, the issue is once you have made the choice of a woman to be with then there would be no more space for friendship with other women. Now you are still driving with a satnav with a female voice, make sure you are not misled. I have to end this letter now. I have so much to do this morning (I started yesterday but only trying to complete it this morning). I will attend mass at 10am then go to the library afterwards. It's getting really busy for now and I hope God guides and leads us in the right direction according to his will and purpose. For now son, stay well, you are blessed, today and always. I look forward to seeing you soon. God bless.

Mum

29.11.18

Dear Son,

I hope this meets you well. Nothing, they say, lasts forever. With only 2 visits a month when you were at B. I wrote more often and looked forward to those visits. Now that we can basically see you every week I now have the freedom to choose. You see, son, everything in life is almost a perspective. Then again M. is not near for me, you know I dislike motorways. The last time, it took me almost 2 hours to get back home. Next time I'll have to leave at 3pm so as to beat the traffic. Yes, everyone is busy and life just goes on. It occurred to me that I had not written in a while. Now that I am writing it's like I'm really not sure what to write about. Anyhow, I only wanted to encourage you to be yourself and the best you can ever be. Nothing, they say, lasts forever. Your sentence was like death to me, now, 4 months on, time is gradually healing the pains and I look to the future with confidence. It's almost Christmas again, and my mind is always fixed on "BY THIS TIME NEXT YEAR". Think of the immense joy and happiness you will feel when your freedom is restored. Again you would not have known the joy of being free until your freedom is taken away from you. Life exists in opposites, and that's just how it is. Whatever it is, joy or sadness, will definitely come to an end. It is in the moment of sadness that we appreciate happiness. Again, it is when we are truly happy that we know what sadness really means. Yeah I'm going to be philosophical now but this shows I'm just trying to fill up the lines on this paper.

I know you have been attending mass regularly, these days, the readings focus on the end of time. People focus on the end of the year and prepare for now to celebrate and usher in the New Year, whether or not they will reach it. The Church on the other hand, talks about the end of time, especially in the book of Revelation or Apocalypse. Scary stuff though, but what is more important for me is my individual end, not the end of the world or rapture as they say.

Remember son, when life gives you pepper, my guy, make pepper soup. May God bless you and keep you, may he make his face shine on you and be gracious to you. May goodness, mercy and favour follow you all the days of your life. Remember you are a house built on the hilltop. You can't be hidden.

God bless you son.

Mum

12.01.19

Dear Son,

It just occurred to me that I have not written you in a long while. I received your letter of the 14th of November yesterday and was wondering why it took two months. Yes, you did explain it had no stamp. Never mind, so many things have happened since then, and I just can't believe that we are already in the long awaited 2019, and from saying "by this time next year" I will say, "by this time this year". Strange too, how this New Year is already 2-week-old. I don't want to bore you with too much details, just to assure you that God is faithful, I strongly believe that not before long you will call me to inform me of your release. I know God is preparing a surprise for me, my joy will be uncontainable when I receive the news, exactly as it was when you gave me the news of your first-class result.

I just can't wait for the appointed time. 2 things happened this week that particularly made me miss you, but at the same time reminded me of what an extraordinary son you are to me. Guess what? A. stumbled into your 'Brothers and Sisters' on YouTube. He said he heard a short conversation in Italian and linked it to me. Can you imagine? He sent me a text to ask if I knew Chris E (as he expected you to be Aweto) He was shocked when I told him you are my son. He loves your music and even wants to visit you. I have been listening to all your music since then. I'm sure you enjoyed the visit of your family today. I hope to see you next week if nothing else comes up. God bless you son – continue to do and be who you've been until now and wait for God to surprise you.

Oh, I still have this space for more ranting. Now something a bit serious which came to my mind in Church yesterday. Please go to confession and start receiving Holy Communion. If you have not already done so.

See you next week.

Mum.

21.01.19

Dear Son,

I know this will meet you well. It was so exciting speaking with you last Friday. Thanks for the call. I am really going to be brief as there's not much to write about. Like I told you over the phone the HO, according to A. has not taken a decision about you. Their strategy is to put a representation forward to prevent them from taking the decision. The main point for now is that you have exercised your treaty right, so not liable to deportation. Your treaty right means that since you obtained your permanent residence in 2010, you never left the country and remained outside the UK for 6 months or more. Son, you have not left this country since 2007, not to talk of staying away for 6 months! To prove this, random letters or certificates are not enough to establish such continuity. That is why it is important to ask your primary, secondary, 6th form and universities to write a statement of attendance confirming the start and end dates. I have written to your universities. I hope to gather everything soon enough to send to A.

Shalom,

Mum.

03.02.19

Arise My Son,

Just took inspiration from today's first reading from the prophet Jeremiah, he said when I was a child I spoke like a child, but now I'm a man. Not sure if the quote is right but that's the idea.

Son, please read the section I wrote on the 1st of February. Somehow, I couldn't get to post this before now, so I felt I could as well maximise the use of this space, after all it's been paid for.

Today I have every reason to thank God as always. Time they say heals everything. It's funny but somehow, I'm used to your being away, I know it is for a purpose and at the appointed time, you will be released. I am already looking forward to that magical moment, can you imagine? By this time ... God knows. I am so happy son, there are things I still can't share with you. Just know that I am happy and that God is truly faithful. Just reflect about today and see how far and how well God has brought us. He will bring the good work he has started in you to completion. I have no doubt that you will endure all the pain now for the sake of the glory that lies ahead. Please look forward to better toilets and facilities.

Mum.

4.03.19

My Dear Son,

I know this will meet you well. Just realised I have not written in a while, I have also not received any letter or telephone call from you. It simply means all is well. I thought I would be able to visit you next Monday, the 11th of March, unfortunately, this will not be possible. I spoke with my mum last Friday. It was the longest conversation I ever had with her. There was no light where she was, so all I could see was her grey hair. She wanted to see you on video but I told her, you were with your family. Yes, I had to hide your situation from her but only to save her more troubles, but thank God, everything has an end. This too shall pass and I just can't wait. I am happy you have been in touch with the Os. I visited them last Saturday and really enjoyed my stay.

M. sends greetings. I was with him last week, he is in his usual self, God really used him to tell me many things. He is looking forward to your release date. As I write this (beginning with green pen) I'm currently in Lewisham Hospital, where I'm currently training as a volunteer Catholic Chaplain to work with patients who are in QE Hospital. Being here reminds me of your first ear operation and how I waited desperately outside, waiting for your recovery. Che tempi ragazzi! Son you have taken me to places, but I have no single regret, God knew my ability to be your mum and that is why he gave you to me as my son. You know what? A worse place to be, worse than being in prison is on a hospital bed, especially after a bereavement. I just hope I'm able, through my volunteering, to give a sense of hope, purpose and meaning to people.

Yes son, Ash Wednesday is here again. It is a time for a new beginning, a time to turn back to him with all our hearts. I really hope you make good use of this, to draw you closer in your relationship with God. I know you are already doing that.

God bless you.

Mum

5.03.19

Arise My Son,

It's Ash Wednesday tomorrow, but it's like I won't be getting any ash as we have parents evening tomorrow. I will keep up with my fasting and abstinence though.

Son, I miss you and I just can't wait for your release date. The waiting makes your release something to look forward to eagerly. Can you imagine?

As things stand, I don't know when next I will see you but know that you are always on my mind. I am here, working and preparing for the day you will be released.

I am also thinking about going back to some of my writing projects, which I left uncompleted.

Please call me on the phone every now and then, if you find the time and of course money. It is better to call the land line which is cheaper. I will update you about your case which, by now should have been presented to the HO by A. I really hope I get to see you soon enough, but whatever the case son know that it is a WIN – WIN situation. There is absolutely nothing to worry about.

I can't believe it's my 3rd month without alcohol. The strange thing is that I never even miss a drink, and the smell of alcohol is really repulsive for me. Yes, maybe I needed all that K's experience and school of life to come to this stage, no experience is wasted.

I have to stop now, Shalom, every peace and blessing.

Mum

3.04.19

Arise My Son,

I can't remember how many times I've tried to sit down to write you without ever doing so, for one reason or the other. I have also been harbouring the stamped envelope in my bag. I have gone to college and returned with it, over and over again. Somehow I kept telling myself that I will return home one of these days to meet you at home. Whatever the case is, the worst has passed, and only the best is yet to come. Too many things to write about but I will see you soon, so you will get the gist live and direct from the horse's/goat's mouth. I just wanted to keep in touch and to encourage you. You have so much demonstrated your strength of character. I can't believe my son will be a 25 year old man in the next days. Almost 8 months have passed son. Can you imagine, your release is closer than ever. Time they say heals everything. Somehow I am conditioned by the fact that we will see soon. I am indeed a fortunate woman, highly favored by God. I know things will work in our favour and to the glory of God.

I'm still dry on alcohol and extremely happy. I only hope I'm able to resist on the day of your release. I just feel it very very near. Thanks for K's birthday card. The boy had a blast, he received many gifts including 15 cards.

Mum.

7.04.19

Arise My Son,

I can't believe I've still not completed this letter. What else? It's Sunday and a bit boring as usual. I'm now on holidays for 2 weeks, so, can see you these two weeks again, I think I'm lazy about writing because I will see you soon. I know I'm doing so much already, but your sentence and absence away from home has made me even the more sensitive to the problems of others. I am now a trained and qualified hospital chaplain, I'm only waiting for my DBS to start. It should be a commitment of 3 hours a week in QE hospital. I am also on the management team of a refugee project which will kick off soon.

It's your birthday this week son, and I can't thank God enough for you. We give God the glory, for the gift of life, for once there is life there is hope, and every other thing follows.

Happy 25th birthday son.
Happy silver celebration.
God bless you today and always.

Mum

15.06.19

Arise My Son,

Happy Sunday son, I know this will meet you well. I woke up this morning to find the picture of a very tall man, standing beside a short man, sent to me by my brother J. "The long and the short" I told myself still half asleep. The Awetos with their intimidating height will always make people look smaller and shorter. When I finally took a proper look this morning I found the two people in the picture are your 2 uncles, the world is a small place. All is set for our trip to Nigeria. Since my last visit to you, I have not been able to erase the image of P. from my memory. First, outside the Iron Gate as we waited to go in, she was so impatient. She kept shaking the gate with all her strength like the gate separated her from something really precious. Then we finally came in, I cannot forget the purest and finest expression of joy on her face when she saw you. I have since then vowed to myself that I would do anything to make and see my granddaughter this happy.

I think I've said all that is needed to be said during my last visit. Just keep having faith while you wait. I am happy that no matter what the future holds, God is in control. We do not know what the future holds but we definitely know who holds the future. My greatest challenge was how you would cope in prison, but you not only coped but are making the best use of it. Consider it a first class in master's degree in self-management and self-discovery. As I write, I only think of the things you have done to make me a proud mother. It is a privilege to be your mother and after these months of incubation, it is a great relief to know that your freedom is nearer with each passing day.

Son, when you pray always ask for the will of God to be done. While expressing your most heartfelt desires to him, know that he knows what is best for you. Take for example V. who has proven to be the ideal woman in every circumstance, and she is doing things that only the woman who is destined to be with you would do. Like I told you, focus on leaving the prison walls first and once outside, things would be sorted out. As I write, I picture the day you would return home. The joy would not in any way be compared to the pain I felt when V. called me on the 18th of August to tell me that you had been taken in. Yes, God allowed the sentence, but before then he had strategically positioned P. and V. in your life. Have you ever thought that your transfer to M. was God's own doing? Have you asked yourself why he took you to a prison so close to where your family can access you easily? By the way son, you have missed nothing, and in spite of your seclusion, you have always had the privilege of seeing your family weekly. I can go on and on, but I just want you to thank God for what you have right now, believing that he who started this would bring it to a successful completion according to his purpose in Christ.

Please, remember these are your last days in the prison. The devil will deal even more deadly blows and God will allow them as your ultimate test of faith. Always try to be vigilant, so that you pass this final test. Do not listen to the stories of other prisoners, for the following reasons:

They are not you, every circumstance is different.

They do not have Pauline Aweto for a mother. My strength comes from the Lord who made heaven and earth.

Remember that HO can only remove you if they can prove that you constitute reasonable/compelling danger to the society/community. You know they cannot prove this, even If you are. So put your heart at peace. And please, do not do anything without consulting your solicitor. They will write to the HO towards the end of July to ask for the outcome of the representations they made 3 months ago.

Hmm ...by this time next year .....

I'm sure you received my post – card from Scotland. The conference was a huge wake up call. I made a lot of connections from South Africa and other African countries including Nigeria. I will not miss the next one coming up in Germany in 2021 but before then, there is another one in Nairobi, Kenya in October this year. I will be acting on some of the decisions I made during the conference when I go to Nigeria. I will keep you updated.

I will so much like to hear your voice before we leave on Thursday, this week, the 20th of June. Our flight leaves at 11:30am. But don't worry if you are not able to, I will understand.

Son, see the Chris in Christ.

Learn from the patience of the dog, he was left to the last, but got the best. Good things come to those who believe, better things to those who are patient, best to those who do not give up. Tenui Nec Dimittam.

Mum

19.06.19

Dear Son,

It was so beautiful hearing your voice yesterday evening. I was very excited and reassured after speaking with you. Your call was a confirmation that the Spirit of the Lord is with us and working in our favour. He led me to return home to receive your call, everything is set and we leave for the airport in 2 hours. I just wanted to drop you these last lines. All I want you to do now is to pray for God's will to be done. I have nothing to lose and everything to gain.

I wanted to share something else with you. I read about a university girl who stabbed her boyfriend (not sure if she killed him). The judge refused to send her to jail because she was very intelligent and bright, so sending her there will "waste" her. Can you imagine? She was allowed to continue her studies and guess what? She dropped out of the university. Can you see that life is not fair and that although all fingers are equal some fingers are more equal? You were sent to jail 2 months after bagging a first-class degree and that made no meaning to the presiding judge. All that is history now. Like I told you yesterday, your solicitor will contact the HO from the 1st of July. I am at peace and so should you. Please remember that you have fought the good fight and have run the race, but to win the prize, you must get to the finishing line. The enemy will intensify his efforts, but make sure you keep your focus on the goal, which is your freedom. Never give any room for a different outcome. Be patient and keep your mind on God. Pray to him and wait for him to answer without asking questions.

I look forward to seeing you soon. God bless and protect you. May he let his face shine on you and be gracious to you.

Shalom.

Mum

1.10.19

Where do I start? Let me start from the new address I wanted to brag with. I didn't know it was going to cost me 9 freaking lines of my writing paper. Can you imagine? It's more than 3 months since I last wrote you, unbelievable but true. So many factors contributed to this. Apart from the scare which arose from what you told me about letters being scrutinised and tested for drugs (I honestly wanted to write in red pen but just remembered that I don't know its potential drug affinity or compatibility or even chemical composition, which by the way I'm also supposed to know so as not to send prohibited substances like the responsible mother I have been "constrained" or socially constructed to be). I'm sure you can feel the difference b/w my teaching in FE and now in HE. Never mind the jargon. More importantly, I think I have come to terms with the reality of your sentence, which is gradually dragging into its logical and most imminent and unavoidable end. This too shall pass away, I initially told myself. Now I can confidently say, this too has passed away.

I reflected over so many things and can only be filled with an attitude of gratitude towards God. Everything in its own time has fallen into place. I am at peace with the entire universe, I am extremely happy and feel fulfilled. God has given me everything, he has not denied me anything. He has intervened in your situation. The HO will not take any further action against you. Be still and know that He is God. Just to let you know how there are different strokes for different folks and how the law is subjectively interpreted, depending on who sits on your case and how lined and deep your pockets are. A woman, can't remember her exact country of origin stole more than 300 million pounds and was caught when she went on a shopping spree where she spent 150 million pounds on a single shopping trip? Know what? She can't be deported to her country because her human rights would be violated. I will not be able to see you again until after my birthday.

Shalom.

Mum

3.10.19

Dear Son,

Son, I had to abandon this again until now. I'm actually in a seminar and I'm enjoying every bit of it. Please call me if you need anything, I am here in Croydon and just a few minutes away from the Home Office. Every Friday, I go for the 12.10 mass. Do you think it is coincidental that the Home Office is sitting right beside a Catholic Church? It is called St' Mary's and I'm sure some of those who come for mass are from that office. It is well.

I just want to remind you that the month of October is also the month dedicated to Mary. I'm currently on the second week of my Marian devotion. Please remember to pray every now and then to turn to her as well. Remember the first miracle of Jesus was at her prompting. I'm struggling to finish this, I have a lecture in 10 minutes so must finish and post by the end of today so that you can receive it on Saturday. Son I'm so much looking forward to the day of your release, A. informed me that he was writing (again) to remind the HO to take a decision, or at least reply his earlier letter. I'm not surprised they are still silent, until they will be obliged by divine injunction and intervention to do the only thing they will do, take no further action. This is my prayer and tomorrow, Friday, I will pass by the HO with the same words of prayer in my heart.

It is accomplished.

Shalom
Pace in terra agli uomini, di buona volontà

Mum

27.10.19

"I have fought the good fight, I have finished the race, I have kept the faith"

2 TIM 4:7

Dear Son,

I just can't get these words out of my mind. I'm sure you heard them at mass today. Yes son, you have fought the good fight and kept faith, you are about finishing your race, awaiting the crown of the righteous God, the only judge.

I am writing you from the central library of Bexleyheath, I came, here after the 8am mass at St Paul's to continue to work on my project I hope to submit it on 1.11.19. It was really nice speaking with you yesterday. Your sentence has really made you a much better person. I refer even to your simple use of language to ask for a favour. Just to let you know that I sent you 200 pounds and your brother in his magnanimity has also sent 100 pounds. You expected 150, almost begging for it, but now you have 300. We bless God. I was with the O's yesterday. I was led by the spirit to go there and you know what? Everyone was home. You can't believe I first buzzed from downstairs and when I got to their floor, I started ringing on the wrong number. Can you imagine? O. had come to get me, we all had a real laugh like those good old days. We also spoke about *bulala* but C. was the only one who didn't know what we were talking about. Would you blame him?

Lest I forget, thanks for the birthday card and the letter you sent me. They came last Wednesday.

As you can see, I'm really struggling to write this, as we have said almost everything either during my last visit or your letter or even the phone. I just want to encourage you because I know it makes you feel good to receive letters from the "outside world" Talking about the outside world, yesterday I listened to some music which says "The city is becoming crappy". Then O. had a T-shirt with "Why you coming so fast" He told me it was about a Turkish visiting the UK for the first time and was hit by a car. I still can't stop laughing even now. I also shared "you've got eyes innit". What can I say on this beautiful Sunday after mass?

Shalom

Saint Mum

1.11.19

"Yahweh will do the fighting for you, you have only to keep still" (Exodus 14:14)

Son, I heard these words in the Church yesterday evening and thought I should share with you. It's the first day of November, the feast of all saints. It is a Holy day of obligation which means it is like Sunday, so all Catholics must go to mass. I'm sure you have mass on this day. I'm only writing to encourage you my son, because God himself will perfect all that concerns you. He has a plan and a purpose for your life and it is in difficulty that we realise how much we really need and depend on him. I just want you to have an open mind and just allow him to fight on your behalf. Remember all that he has done for you in the past? Remember the letter from student finance? Yes, that's exactly how it will be. I really have to stop now, as I have to get ready to go to work. May God bless and protect you, may he let his face shine on you and be gracious to you. He is your strength. Hold on to him and let him surprise you, yes he will surprise you.

Mum

23.11.19

Arise My Son,

Words fail me as I sit down to write this missive. By the way missive is another word for letter. I have not checked whether or not it is right, or better, if still in use. Whatever. The day has been exceptionally eventful, starting with your call this morning. You made my day, even as early as 9.30am. I just went back to bed and only came to the library a few minutes ago. The funny thing is that all the computers have been shut down, which means I can't even work. But I discovered why God wanted me to come out at this time of the day. I ran into a woman I used to meet at the 7.30 mass in Erith, before going to work. We had so much to share, and there is so much I can do for her. In her words, "I'm 70 and still working, what for?" Now with the computers down, I am seizing the opportunity to write. As you can see, my hand writing is not jittery, because I am the happiest person in the world right now. I am happy because I am blessed to have a son like you, I am happy your experience, rather than break you is making you a much better and more determined person.

Just Thursday I was in a shop in Beckenham and I swear I heard your song being played. It is the second time this is happening to me. Like it or not God is using everything to our advantage and we will finally attain that joy and happiness that only knowing and working in his will and purpose can give us. I just wanted to share this with you that nothing happens by chance. We only need to have faith to believe that all things work together unto good to them that love the Lord and are called according to his purpose. (Romans 8:28). As we prepare for another Christmas, I just expressed a secret wish to *babbo natale. Esiste ancora? Ma certo che esiste.* This Sunday is the last Sunday of the year and we celebrate Christ as the King of the universe. Let him reign in your life and you will see the difference. You will be naturally high like I have been for almost a year now. It is a state of perfect peace that only He can give. Once you have it, nothing can take it away from you. It makes you thrive where others strive.

By this time... only God knows how perfect and complete my joy would be. Your sentence is coming to an end, yes son, you have fought the good fight, and you have finished the race. All you are waiting for now is the crown which God, in his faithfulness will give you. He will give you freedom because your destiny lies only with him. He will give you freedom without conditions. Always remember that whoever has been set free by the son of man, is free indeed. Sunday, the 1st of December will be the first Sunday of Advent. Advent is a time of waiting and expectation for the birth of the child Jesus. I have waited and as I enter this season I do so with great expectations, and so should you.

Mum

20.01.2020

Dear Son,

Can you imagine? I was just contemplating how to write a final letter to finally seal the end of this journey that started like a nightmare. Strangely, you had the same idea to write me and this time, you beat me to it. You wrote me first, now I'm struggling to reply, but nothing will stop me. Where do I start? Somehow, I'm only writing to fulfil all righteousness but I really feel different now, especially as I know that the end is in sight. When last I visited you on the 28th of December, I felt that was the last time I would see you behind those frozen walls. It is exactly the same way I feel now. To reply to this letter, I had gone back to re-read some of the letters you sent me in the past. The very first one was written on the 6.9.18. Time has gone by and as they say there is nothing time cannot heal. We have come a long way and still find it hard to believe that victory at last is ours. You have fought the good fight and the will of the good Lord for the purpose of your life has not been in vain. It has prevailed against every mitigating circumstance. Back to your last and final letter, all I can say is that no matter how you wish to re-enact your triumphant exit, I have only one thing to tell you. Make sure you leave as soon as those massive doors open into the outside world. If time expires and you find yourself closed on the wrong side, then that I suppose will be your business. Don't over dramatise your exit, JUST DO IT. Whatever you are coming out with, in boxes, bags or cartons, just remember all my letters to you, which I will need for a project. I will explain this further upon your release. NFA – No further action. I will remember this and update what NFA means for most Nigerians – no future ambitions – Son, as we come to the end of this ordeal, I have only one hymn to sing to the Lord, it is the Magnificat, or the Song of Mary.

My soul glorifies the Lord,
My spirit rejoices in God my Saviour,
He looks on his servant in her lowliness.
Henceforth, all generations shall call me blessed.
The Almighty has done great things for me,
Holy is his name, his mercy is from age to age, on those who fear him,
He puts forth his arm in strength and scatters the proud hearted,
He casts the mighty from their thrones and raises the lowly,
He feeds the starving with good things – sends the rich away empty, he protects Israel his servant remembering his mercy, the mercy promised to our fathers, to Abraham and his sons forever.

Fine

E vissero felici e contenti

14

Letters from My Son

6.09.18

Dear Mama,

Dearest and greatest of all mamas!! Oh! I am so happy your letter cheered me up this morning. I am thankful to hear that you and K are doing fine. As for myself, I am coping very well in this "five-star hotel" in which they placed me. It is good to be good, in fact, it is even better when we do not dwell over our past misfortunes, especially our quarrels over Sunday mass, therefore I am thankful that you do not miss them.

As a matter of fact, I was actually at mass on the 21st and 22nd Sundays in ordinary time. I promised myself to keep the Sabbath holy after finishing with my studies. The priest here offered me a bible, I chose the one written in Italian so as my spirit continues to journey further into growth, so does my knowledge of Italian. You are right mum, things could be worse.

If you are apologising for preaching to me in your letter, I don't accept it. I am your son and cannot grow without your wisdom. I hope to come out a better person. I can only imagine that eagles have hundreds of feathers in their lifespan. With each day that goes by, I pluck one of my feathers so as to make space for new ones to grow.

As the days pass the old me fades away into darkness and the new me comes to light.

Royal mail need not only earn your money but also your respect. For you are one of many queens from our home land. Speaking of which! Royal mail needs to deliver a gold jubilee to my grandma! They also need to keep the platinum one on standby ready to be signed, sealed and delivered!

Since my being here I have gained the inspiration to write a novel as a creative artist, one of my dreams has become to release our next books at the same time, same story with different perspectives.

Thank you so much for your letter, mum. With your words of encouragement, I grow in peace with God. Nevertheless, there is never a time when the devil is not at work. There is a strange threat that I encountered two weeks ago.

Somebody from the HO came to me on the 5th. She told me that I am liable for deportation under the regulation of the EEA laws 2016. She told me I have 20 days to produce a letter with evidence, stating why the decision should not be made against me. She said my conviction provoked this investigation and I would be deported back to Italy.

There is a lot of work to be done, but like you said mum, no matter the circumstance, my expectation remains great. I have already made plans for the worst-case scenario but I await for the Lord's revelation, expecting the worst and hoping for the best.

Thank you, mum,

God bless you too.

9.09.18

Dearest Mother,

Thank you for your letter, your hopes have been fulfilled for your letter found me well. I tried to reply on the same day, but I was too busy, LOL yes that's right too busy in prison, can you imagine. I went for mass this morning but we only practised our communion rites, this is because our priest has taken leave for 4 weeks. I of course did not receive for I felt I was not in the state of grace, nevertheless, I kept the weekly sheet for my private study. I have 3 sheets now and once I have 72 of them, I will be free.

Anyway mum, forget that. I'm so thankful for your life and that of our family. No matter whatever God has in store for us it will all work unto good, I look forward to seeing you soon.

God bless you too.

30.09.18

Happy Sunday Mum,

Earlier today I spoke to you over the phone and was delighted to hear your voice. Shortly after being locked up again, I received a letter from you which was dated the 23rd of this month. I believe this must be what you wrote lastly before departing for your conference in Italy.

You will struggle to believe the joy our conversation brought to my inner peace, for the whole week, I have been speculating how much *wahala* HO must have put you through in gathering and delivering those evidences.

Anyway, the reading which you quoted from the book of Wisdom did speak to me in a few ways. Reflecting over the way I felt last week whilst writing my letter to you, I remember how I felt. The way the immigration staff spoke to me felt as though I was in a den of hissing serpents all trying to derail me with their misinformation.

Reading further into your letter, my theories were confirmed, you will never stop or pause for a moment in battle for your own children. I said to myself, that this is the extent of my mother's unconditional love.

The mention of your conference reminds me of the first time I ever saw you on TV, myself, dad, K and granny were watching you and back then, to see a black woman passionately speaking on TV was simply unheard of.

This is where your efforts belong, where you feel you can contribute passionately and freely with no expectations. I just felt that with this burning desire to raise awareness on human trafficking that your fighting these people would have grounded you indefinitely.

I hope upon the day of my release that I will be able to align my dreams with your mission and contribute with my creative ideas. You are my greatest inspiration as an artist and a writer mother. I am forever thankful for this.

I look forward to writing back to the letters you have written. May God bless you always mum.

7.10.18

Greetings, I received two of your letters yesterday. Here I am writing to you on a Sunday afternoon for the consecutive third week now. These moments that I spend writing to you are my most peaceful, they always follow a warm and fruitful mass service.

11.10.18

Dear Mum,

You may get this letter some days after but hopefully if you are home from Italy, you will hear from me. I'm thrilled that you find encouragement through your writings to me, After all, if there is something that God has called you to do, it is to be an inspiring writer.

I am happy that on the day of our visit you met me a calm and confident person. As I mentioned earlier, your inspiring letters are what made me the courageous man that stood before you that day.

I am also overjoyed knowing that you now see me as the righteous son I have been trying desperately to become. I strongly believe now that you and I can both see that our intentions towards each other are pure.

There is a lot to be done mother, as I write to you, I am trying to maintain my spiritual balance through this period of trial and turbulence. I am well health wise, but I feel that the pressure of this investigation is making me uncomfortably anxious and it is becoming increasingly difficult to manage the stress as the weeks go by.

In the demise of my weakness, I still have your strength and for that I remain strong and reflectful. I hope you will be able to appreciate the reason for my troubles as I continue to write, but also as I write, I feel a great spirit revealing to you and I, a perspective that promotes great favour from God, please bear with me as I continue to explain.

At this time of confusion and complications as you mentioned in your letters mum, I would consider us to paint the bigger picture and consider our options as far as our minds can think. I for a long time have been a stubborn child but now I try to act as far and wide from the margin as I possibly can.

My questions throughout the weekend, what do we gain by fighting this case that will fulfil our spiritual efforts? So far we have been praying for my freedom and safety. There is a sign as I walk past every Sunday saying BE SMART! YOUR FAMILY WANTS YOU TO GET OUT ON TIME. In addition, the more I see it the more I feel we are giving HO the power to keep me inside with our efforts to fight their decisions.

Does it make sense to risk or sacrifice our righteous energies for a case that so early on is already defined? We stand a very good chance but whatever the worth of our chances we can still lose this appeal and after a long time of fighting still end up with the short straw.

But in hindsight of all this, I have tried to be as objective as possible to weigh out our options. But if we allow the enemy to play its last, worst and final card, we can refocus. Like I said: Peacemakers, when they work for peace, sow the seeds which will bear fruits in holiness.

All of this I write, remembering the day you told me about seeds, how one from a fruit can be used to grow a tree bearing many fruits. Anyway, mum, no matter what, I will obey your every counsel, as I believe you have been my advisor in all these things. I on the other hand believe I don't belong here if prison remains my prospect for longer than the time I will serve.

21.10.18

Dear Mum,

Happy Sunday once again.

Last week Sunday, I was actually invited to do the first reading, because of that I am quite familiar with what you described in your letter. I was also invited to Stations of the Cross the Friday beforehand, it was here where the priest and some others complimented me for my eloquent speech and invited me to do Sunday reading. I am in upmost agreement with you on the value of wisdom. I listened throughout the Gospel reading and homily and felt very happy after leaving mass. I was actually drawn by the way in which the priest described wisdom, as a combination or amalgamation of knowledge, education and experience. in my reading routine, Confucius, a Chinese administrator in a court who lived some time before Christ (556BCE), also struck me.

His simple, yet philosophical saying made me enthusiastic about my journey 'what you know you know, what you don't know, you don't know'. This is true wisdom. On the topic of reading, I received the books you brought me, rest assured they would be masticated and digested well (in the context of information that is).

God bless you too.

28.10.18

Dearest Mother,

Thank you so much for your letter, I met it in high spirits, I was actually busy reading a book before I noticed your envelop next to my cell door. I thank you also for the great passage you wrote for me, it gives me strength and courage to know that you are well versed in the word of God. This makes me look forward to my future with great promise.

I was pleased to hear how delighted you were in learning about my transfer to M., definitely, it was a blessing that came directly from God. Before they called me to give me the news, I was already up, however, I was expecting to be sent to the education department, so I was quite surprised to hear I was being moved. Before leaving my cell, I made the sign of the cross and thanked God for granting me the place where I dwelt, already I felt so much stronger and so much wiser for this path that was chosen for me.

Believe it or not V. actually dreamt about my transfer to a closer prison. Can you imagine? She was upset when she couldn't book a visit but she was excited when she learnt of my transfer, like the English people say "Bless her cotton socks". I will be able to see her and P. more often here in this prison; I will tell you more about the toilets and facilities on our next visit.

Today we went for mass, my inmates and I, it was beautiful, it reminded me of the day of Pentecost being together in Church with people from different countries. The Gospel was about a miracle Jesus performed when a blind man called out to him in a crowd. The homily is actually quite relatable with the expression you wrote in German, but please it is too long for me to mention in this letter.

Anyway mum, once again I'm happy for your letter, I am looking forward to seeing you soon, please take care and continue to stay blessed until then.

God bless you too.

31.10.18

Dearest Mother,

Reading what you wrote on the 18th made me reflect over our trials and tribulations. We have really been pushed by the devil yet he gained no inch. I too am filled with joy in knowing how much happiness and how much peace you felt on the day before your birthday. I too am happy with the progress I have made since my accident because I know that God has truly blessed my efforts.

Sometimes I wonder how our sufferings are so easily forgotten like when you finish an exam after cramming for the whole night and you don't even remember what you wrote.

4.01.19

Dear Mum,

Thank you so much for your last visit, each time I am greeted by the motherhood trilogy, I find myself greatly humbled.

During these months of incubation, I have reflected a lot and God has guided me to the revelations I needed to experience only when the time was right. I am sure I don't need to tell you this because you know already, nevertheless mother, I believe you were blessed with a curious and inquisitive soul and those traits are very much alive in me and P.

Our lack of patience comes from our strong desire to know what happens next, where God wants us to be we just want to be there. I was barely four years of age when I asked you about heaven and death, it is no surprise people often refer to me as a 'deep diver' that is someone who enjoys to search for the deeper meanings in life.

As I am slowly reaching the final terms of my sentence, in looking back, I noticed how many times I could have perished, yet God was always there to protect me. So many times, I have thought of how things have strategically ended up in my favour. At this point, I can only express how happy I am to be alive; I strongly believed God allowed the sentence to pass because he knew I could manage it.

God has taught me that whilst the circle of humanity lives on, glory will always come at a price, if I was unable to obtain the glory of my graduation, perhaps God would have intervened in my sentencing, can you imagine?

On the other hand, what could have been better could have been worse and what is worse can only get better. Upon my release, I will still be a graduate; no evil instance can ever revoke the moment you shouted with joy in learning the height of my success. It is safe to say that was only the beginning.

I am beginning to notice the changes in the season as the weather grows warmer and warmer, I realise my final months in here are getting nearer and nearer. It's hard to imagine by this time next year I will be free, only God knows what he has in stock for me but it feels to me that great things lie ahead for us all.

I feel ready for any challenge the devil has thrown at me. I did not carry my bible with me to custody for a reason. At the same time, I appreciate how I am born of a nation that will always fall short of God's glory and I must take heed in every step of what is left of my sentence.

I received your post cards some weeks ago before your letter arrived. I added it to a collection of cards you sent me earlier in April 'Grow through what you go through', 'shine bright like a diamond' ' never never never give up' are all glued to my wall. It may make you lough to know I used prison issue toothpaste as glue, a trick many residents here use to stick photographs of women in their cell.

I look forward to your return from Nigeria. By then it will be just over six months left to my sentence. It is well mamma, shalom and God bless.

God bless you too.

20.04.19

Dearest of all Mothers,

I was reading my 2018 diary to see what I was getting up to on my birthday. Last year, that was the day after I recorded my project video in the studio. I feel very joyful reflecting over those days, they remind me how my temporary defeat in prison was no match for the victory that came beforehand. I already made my mother so proud.

In fact, it was as though the devil momentarily forgot to strike and, in a panic, pushed an emergency button. I remember how I felt when I went to go and get my result, I actually never had the time to bask in the glory, I just needed to rush home to show you my result and wao! What a proud moment it was for me when I said; here you go mum, I have finished the race.

I often wonder what I will accomplish next that will bring out a reaction like the one you displayed when I got my result; you have no idea how happy I was to see you that way. I'm not sure you will remember what I am about to tell you but there was a conversation I remember having with you where I promised that all your efforts will be rewarded in the end, it was just a question of time.

I can honestly say my graduation was merely a testimony of the greater miracles that are yet to come and I honestly cannot wait to show you what your son is capable of.

I was actually performing one of my songs to a crowd of people at the chapel on Wednesday... a spirit moved me to start rapping, if only you could see the looks on people's faces.

I read or better still, I narrated the passion of our Lord Jesus according to Luke on Palm Sunday and John on Good Friday. The feedback I received very much inspired me to one day read at the cathedral in the Vatican, it was awesome.

Shalom mother, God bless you too.

11.01.20

Dear Mum,

Like the goodness and kindness that followed us all the days of our lives, I am sure this letter will find you well.

I am writing this as a means of signing off this long and eventful journey, this will be the last letter that I write to you before I am released and I cannot deny that right now, I feel awesome.

I have been making my best efforts to prepare for my departure; sadly, I am finding time to progressing a little too quickly.

I mean for goodness sakes, you should see how much time I have wasted reflecting on the means by which I should pack my belongings. I said to my friends I want to come out looking presidential, one of them said 'by which method do you intend to look presidential when you will be walking out of a prison carrying cardboard boxes? The other one said well, boxes or bags does not matter, as I'm sure some Ghanaians were not given their bags in the past yet they had to go.

It's funny how things have tuned out honestly, spending all this time thinking of how to get out of here as soon as possible, but now that that day is fast approaching, it's as if I no longer wish to leave in a hurry.

I consider myself very blessed to have received that letter of no further action. One person actually came to me two days ago to tell me only the luckiest of people receive an NFA, as it is the highest and most rare of blessings that one could receive in this prison.

In any case, mum, I am very happy to be alive and very happy to be coming home in the next month. None of this would have been possible without God, but without you supporting me throughout this time, He would have needed an angel to save me. Thank you so much for your love and support, *ti voglio tanto bene mamma.*

PART III

REFLECTIONS:
LESSONS FROM LIFE

15

On the Inevitability of Change

'You cannot enter the same river twice' or everything is in a state of flux was the conclusion some of the early Greek philosophers (especially Heraclitus) came to as they grappled with understanding and explaining the concept of change and being.

We live with change, it happens all the time, it is so present in our lives that we sometimes ignore it. But that doesn't make it disappear, especially when things appear stable and comfortable. We simply believe or rather assume that it will last for ever, so we are never prepared when the unexpected happens.

But the question is, was this unexpected? Or that we choose not to expect it?

It is interesting that, on the contrary, we assume that things will change for the better when the odds are against us. In both cases, whether we expect change or not, most people hardly take the conscious decision to plan to mitigate against those eventualities when they show up, unannounced and unwelcomed.

In human relationships, separation, death, disease or even divorce are all possible alterations that many are not prepared to face until they happen. Women are most likely to be affected. With the separation from a partner or even death, they find themselves carrying the burden of caring for their children alone. This is even more difficult if they depended exclusively on them.

I've also realised that with the passage of time that change is not in every person's vocabulary, that, as a matter of fact, there are people who are immune to change. In such cases, love is never enough and hope will just not cut it. Faith may come into play, but more as believing and accepting the evidence before our eyes.

True enough, planning for change is not enshrined in the African DNA. But the sooner we initiate those difficult conversations as reasonably practicable the better for us. Change must happen, the more prepared we are, the better we are able to cope.

As difficult as it may appear at first, I've learnt that change could be a great time for growth and development. If fully embraced without the negative connotations it evokes, it could be a wakeup call to face issues we've swept under the carpet for so long. It could also be an open invitation to explore new horizons, challenge ourselves to come out from our comfort zone and face the unknown.

For people like me who thrive on routine, stability and predictability, change could be devastating, especially if we do not seek it actively. For most people, change happens as an imposition of a higher force or order beyond their control. I feel that if we are all given the opportunity to change, most of us will never do so, at least consciously and deliberately. Maybe this was why we needed the Covid 19 to usher in a new world order of the 'new normal' in a way that we had no choice but to adapt.

16

On the Here and Now, the There and After

I've come to understand that it is crucial that we do not become too comfortable with where we are, here and now, good or bad as it may seem. I've learnt and paid a very high price for being comfortable with where I was, my here and now, without making adequate provision for the there and after. Comfort in the here and now breeds complacency, a red flag for lack of motivation and consequent deficit in productivity, creativity, and overall effectiveness. For people who are no longer excited about where they are now, it might be a sign that they possibly need that much dreaded change. There are two options: either they actively seek this change or it will happen anyway. Reflecting on my personal experience, I still find it unbelievable that I was in one job role for eleven years. There were opportunities to progress through internal vacancies. As a loyalist, it was just enough for me to excel in what I did without seeking recognition or even promotion. For me, teaching was simply an act of service to humanity, "to the least of my brothers and sisters, who didn't have the same opportunity and privilege of education I had", I often told myself.

Complacency made me resistant to change. I didn't see it coming even when it constituted a 100% of the air I breathed. It was difficult for me to spot the red flags for one reason: I found my purpose and fulfilment in what I did. I discovered a new vocation to support women to progress in their careers through skills development and subsequent enrolment into higher education. For me, it had always been about supporting women at different levels of vulnerability. Nevertheless, it seemed I forgot myself in the process of taking care of others. I've learnt that I must put on my life jacket and oxygen mask first before I attempt to help others, as I am constantly reminded each time, I board a flight. I took flights regularly and heard these words time and time again. They never made any sense to me, until a very dear friend brought this to my attention.

But change happened in my here and now. All at once, all I'd worked to build, sustain and defend across eleven long years became irrelevant. Profit was prioritised over people, qualification over skills, and pursuit over purpose. Funding became the driving force for curriculum development. Second chances to adults were significantly slashed and pushed to the back seat to give way to young people's first chance. A new leadership emerged, with a focus on values totally different from the same values and principles that kept me glued to one place for this length of time.

Yes, change happened. I didn't see it coming. Maybe, a better expression is that I didn't want to see it.

Reflectively, there were red flags I should've captured in my self-righteousness. I'd coped with discomfort and absorbed high levels of stress and anxiety that I could've recognised as symptoms of an underlying "dis-ease". But I kept on for convenience, my number one enemy to change. I kept fitting in when I no longer fitted. I felt like the ground I stood on was removed from right under my feet. It was an extremely stressful and emotionally draining time. I couldn't believe I could be this 'disposable' and dispensable. I was at a minus-zero point. I took a back seat to watch my entire career replay in front of me like

I was watching a home movie. Self-guilt and doubt were other strong emotions that I had to deal with. Was it worth it after all? Did I really belong there?

Providentially, I had other more pressing issues to handle at the time. My motherhood was being tested too. The choice between my role as a mother and my position as a lecturer was unmistakably clear.

Six months later, I felt I was ready to return to work. Education remained my passion and calling. But I wasn't going to make the same mistake twice. I wasn't ready to pay a similar price, with or without a discount. This time around, I wanted to choose where I wanted to be, consciously and strategically, with both short- and long-term goals. I never again wanted to leave anything to chance. I wanted to make my own choices rather than just take chances. To start with, I had to discount convenience and comfort. I had to stretch and challenge myself to go the distance and put myself 'out there', one of the few things I passionately disliked.

While I still find fulfilment in my work, I am consciously mindful of the next steps to take. I realised I needed to be seen to be believed, rewarded, and recognised. To be honest, I found this difficult. In a way, this was against my nature and Catholic upbringing. My *modus operandi* was to follow the biblical injunction of not letting my left hand know what my right hand did. I guess I must have misunderstood humility to mean invisibility. I didn't want to receive my reward here on earth, but I soon understood that the way of the world is different. Contrary to my belief, it was not enough to go above and beyond to consistently exceed expectations in my personal and more essentially, professional targets. Didn't the bible say that 'no one lights a lamp to put it under a tub, they put it on a lampstand where it shines for everyone in the house?' (Matt 5:15-16). Let your light shine before men so that they may see your good works and give glory to your father in heaven. I wish I had understood this much earlier in life, that God does find glory in our good works when men "see" them.

From experience, I discovered that I needed to constantly remind myself of my targets and goals. I had to be intentionally ambitious. Consequently, I stepped up the leadership ladder in less than a year. This was a huge eye opener for me. As a programme leader, I could be the change I wanted to see, steer the ship where I wanted it to go, provide vision and deliver strategies, have more impact and influence through responsibility of management and mentorship of academic staff.

Four years later, what I previously desired as my 'there and after' has, for some time now become my 'here and now'. My heart continues to yearn for greater opportunities for impact and influence as the wind of change continues to blow over me. My restlessness of heart, my quest for new opportunities and experiences is best expressed by St Augustine in his Confessions – "You stir man to take pleasure in praising you- Because you have made us for yourself and our heart is restless until it rests in you".

17

On Self-Knowledge

As a person, I see myself ear-marked by destiny in a way that is compelling and totally beyond my control. In my inward journey of self-discovery, I found out that I am privileged to be part of the 15 to 20% of the world's population defined by psychology as a Highly Sensitive Person (HSP). Such people, like me are very emotional, compassionate, generous, sensitive and feel different from everyone. Putting psychology aside, I believe I inherited compassion and generosity from my mother. I must have pushed this a step further through discovering how passionate I am about helping people, which is like a second nature to me. Sometimes I feel overwhelmed about how very far I am willing to go just to help someone in need. Sacrificing myself and my comfort for the benefit of others, irrespective of vulnerability is the most natural thing for me to do, even without thinking about it. I don't have to make any effort to be good to others. On the contrary, I would really need to make effort to be mean to people. In such instances, I would be acting against my own nature. I would be giving people the privilege to control my reaction.

One main idea I embraced from the philosophy of Socrates is that self-knowledge is the height of knowledge. Knowing me has been a long and continuous journey, through different phases and stages. I'm work in progress and the final version of me has not fully enfolded. In the meantime, I enjoy all that have impacted my life positively. Every day, I wake up to embrace a new and better version of me, which, essentially, involves my acceptance of change as part of my journey. Such changes have helped me to grow, evolve, redefine, and rebrand myself, while remaining the same person I've always been. Knowing myself has enabled me to make choices and changes in my life that are in alignment with my character, personality, strengths, beliefs, limitations and most importantly, purpose, which permeates all other aspects of my life.

In my quest for self-knowledge, I've discovered my purpose, why God created me exactly the way I am and what he wants to use me for. I like to see myself as a tool or an instrument, made in an explicit way, for a defined purpose to solve explicit problems, at a particular time, place and space. To meet the person specification God used in defining me, I can't be anyone else, I must know, embrace and accept me for who I am. Sometimes I wished I was different – not always and everywhere in the 'straight and narrow' and always striving to know and do the right thing. Sometimes I wished I can choose to do the wrong thing, at least just to have the satisfaction of knowing exactly what it feels to be on the wrong side of the fence, at least once. But I feel that just once may be more than enough to compromise my destiny and derail my purpose.

Essentially, I consider myself a minimalist. For me, less is more and more is superfluous. I'm not an acquaintance of consumerism. I have a very practical and functional relationship with materialism. My personal interests are driven by purpose, value and meaning. I don't value objects simply because of the price tag they carry, who carries them or whether they are 'trending' in any social media platform. Over time, I've learnt that placing value on things is subjective, depending on the worth people place on them and the price they are willing or able to pay for them, according to their financial capability. On the contrary the value I place on principles and virtues such as integrity, commitment, compassion and honesty is priceless.

Embracing simplicity is me in my element. It is also a conscious choice that I make on a daily basis. Simplicity as a choice of lifestyle does not come cheap or easy. Discipline and detachment have helped me greatly to persist in a simplified approach to life which fully expresses and reflects my personality in its originality. Being simple isn't that simple. It also comes at a price, like every choice we make. As a choice, it means preference, giving up something in other to select another. It also involves a process of rationalisation and analysis, weighing up the benefits and finding responses to the heaps of "whys", "why nots", "if nots", "then whats" and "so whats". Most of the time we tend to be very impulsive in our decision making, often allowing emotions and what we feel at the time to becloud our judgement. If we are honest with ourselves, we soon realise that we may feel differently about the same situation in a different circumstance and time. If only we think a little bit deeper, we would realise that our desire for an object ends the very moment we acquire it, and it becomes old the first time we ever use it. What is more, the cycle begins all over again. Media and advertisement know just how to tempt us with updates and new features and gadgets that soon make our newly acquired products obsolete.

I've never taken the power of choice for granted. I consider it a rare privilege to be able to make conscious, intentional choices and decisions, irrespective of surrounding situation, environment and perceived open invitation to change. Friendship, for example, is one area of life where choice and change have been inevitable for me. I have come to realise that all friendships are not meant to last a lifetime as we tend to believe. Sometimes we want to massage our ego and take pride in parading a lifetime friendship or relationship, when all the time it had been on life support. We are socialised, especially as Africans to place more value on the length of a relationship rather than the quality. This happens also with our focus on how long people live rather than how well they lived. I believe that reasons and seasons apply to friendship. It is entirely up to us to decipher when the season is over and the reason no longer hold. Nevertheless, true and worthy friendship will stand the test of time and remain changeless with every wind of change. As I progressed in life, I realised that some people I initially considered to be an indispensable part of my journey can no longer be part of it, either because we no longer share the same destination, routes to take or even baggage allowance that would determine our mode of transportation. Friends who do not contribute to our progress are often more than just place holders. It is logical that if they do not help to move us forward, they simply help to bring us back, by making us remain where we are. In my life, I've realised how the person specification for the job of friendship has changed over time. Although sharing same values and principles have always determined my choice of friends, I have updated this to include those who would help me grow and develop personally, professionally, spiritually as well as those who have a positive approach to life and inspire me to be more and do more. Mastering how to manage my expectations has helped me to discern who I accommodate and give access to my time and resources. The more I grow, with the passage of time, the more my desire and taste for friendship change. Friendship, as I have come to understand is a double-edged sword. It can be a tool for change as well as an obstacle to progress and the growth we all desire.

I have understood that I need to know who I am to be who I want to be. Knowing me also puts me in a better position to know others as well. I've learnt not to understand people without first knowing them. Trying to understand the people I don't know is a glorified form of tolerance. While the knowledge I have of them will last and justify the way I treat and approach them, tolerance alone won't last. It has a limit and an expiration date, sometimes around the corner. Understanding, more than tolerance could form the basis for a long lasting and fruitful relationships.

Oftentimes, we try to change other people. This is one area I think I have failed. But my failure in trying to change people has taught me an important and unforgettable lesson. If I want to be successful in changing others, there is only one way – change myself, or at least my attitude or perception of them. People also don't realise that it is easier to change themselves than to change others. Often, they expect the other to be the initiator of change due to pride and prejudice. Again, many people find it difficult to change so they pass the responsibility to others. One of the greatest lessons my mother taught me is, if I want something done quickly, I must do it myself. Although this significantly affected my ability to develop my delegation skills as I progressed in my work life, I have found this advice applicable in my interpersonal relationships as well. It is another way of being the change I desire to see in others. It is a win-win situation for me. Every time I change, I discover that I become a better me. I become stronger. My inner self is fed and nourished. My flesh is starved as I reap the fruits of discipline and stretch and challenge myself beyond my limits and comfort zone.

18

On Happiness and Joy

Most religions, if not all, build on the search for happiness as the main purpose of our existence. Others have even pushed it a step further, to include happiness as our purpose for the life hereafter, other than life, here and now. Happiness, contrary to what we believe is not a destination but a journey. Those with this mistaken concept of happiness often miss the mark and spend their entire life chasing after happiness. They often do not even realise when they arrive at their destination of happiness, because the pursuit of happiness has become their goal, which keeps shifting and prevents them from enjoying life, moment after moment. Words used to define happiness include 'seeking after', striving, moving towards the achievement of a better or even perfect life. We often equate 'better' with 'more'. Western culture and its agenda to promote materialism has successfully and systematically convinced us that better means more – more cars, money, fame, success, perfect body image, perfect marriages, and relationships. All these concepts are mis-sold to us as ideal. Those in the real world know there is nothing like a perfect life or relationship. We can only take what our reality as it is and make it ideal or pretend it is ideal. Social media is the common marketplace to showcase our ideal lifestyles, relationships, and possessions. We are all constantly encouraged and reminded to fake our realities or even 'manifest' them to make them real.

If happiness is a desired goal, an aspiration for a better and more perfect life, it means that it is never permanent. We can understand this better when we understand happiness as essentially tied to temporary feelings and moments of excitement, fun and delirium linked to external events, people, places or even tangible things as the underpinning sources or fountain of our delight. From personal experience, I've learnt that happiness too is a choice, a decision and a matter of the mind.

Essentially, happiness as a choice comes at the price of individual responsibility without the possibility of delegation to someone else. 'He/she makes me happy', we often hear people say. For the majority, this is enough to mortgage a whole lifetime. Experience too has taught me that feelings can change depending on our mood.

Happiness as a decision means it is intentional and deliberate. Often, it doesn't happen by chance.

Happiness as a state of mind encompasses both choice and decision as correlating factors. It is, contrary to what we believe, not an issue of the heart but of the inner mind, contentment, freedom and a real sense of detachment.

Although 'instances' of pleasure may make us happy, happiness is not pleasure itself, but our individual ability to adapt to our external circumstances and manage our expectations.

One choice I have made in life, is the personal decision not to take the risk of delegating my happiness to another person or object. In life, we believe that certain persons, relationships or things are responsible for our happiness. This is specifically true of a marriage relationship, where a person's reason for wanting to marry an individual is simply because he or she makes him/her happy by doing a specific thing or behaving in a specific manner. However, years later, the same things that made them happy would become irritating and even boring. We all change, with time, as well as the things and attention which make us happy. It is like watching the same movie over and over again and expect the same reaction as if it was the first time it was being seen.

A decision to be happy means that I am not conditioned by surrounding circumstances or how people behave towards me or even threat me. My happiness is my responsibility and if I decide to allow people to condition my happiness, it means I have given them the power to control how I feel or even think. I've learnt that this is a dangerous place to be.

Joy, though sometimes used as a synonym of happiness, is different. It comes from within. Unlike happiness, it is not conditioned by external circumstances, feelings, events or even people. It comes from the inside as an inner state of mind. Joy defies individual status, education or wealth. As a Catholic, I prefer the spiritual or biblical perspective of joy as one of the numerous 'fruits' of the Holy Spirit. Fruits are the products of the gifts when activated by faith. Apart from joy the other fruits of the Holy Spirit are love, peace, forbearance, kindness, goodness, faithfulness, gentleness and self-control (Gal 5: 22-23). The gifts, on the other hand are wisdom, understanding, counsel, fortitude knowledge, piety and the fear of the Lord (Is 11:1-2).

19

On Prayer and Life in the Spirit

Prayer has remained constant in my everyday life. From early childhood I've been taught to pray. However, the way I pray has significantly changed over the years. The more I grow and go deeper in my relationship with God, the more my reason and attitude to prayer also change. Increasingly, I've grown from using prayer as a simple wish list to inform God of all that I legitimately demand as rightfully mine, to an understanding of prayer as a request to change what I want, to conform to his will. In doing so, I'm constantly reminded of Jesus' model prayer; 'give us this day our daily bread' or 'give us today our daily bread'. "Lord for tomorrow and its needs I don't pray..." is a classical hymn that readily comes to mind as well.

I learnt and embraced prayer as an essential part of my daily life, both from the Catholic Church and more from the religious life. Praying the Liturgy of the Hours or the universal prayer of the Church makes me feel the oneness of humanity and gives me the sense of belonging to a universal family, approaching God in prayer, simultaneously, from different parts of the world, using the same words and praying for the same intentions. Using the same scripture readings and intercessions with over four billion people gives me that spirit of connectedness, to people with a common purpose, on the same journey and destiny.

Like every other person I have sometimes become lukewarm, with the routine of prayer, often reciting with my lips or mouth, with my mind and heart so far away. At such moments, I feel like one of those whom Christ says honour him with their lips but with their hearts are far away. (Matt 15:8)

There have been instances in my life where I desperately 'needed' God to answer my prayers – urgently, exactly the way I wanted it and when I wanted it. It was like I was his counsellor and personal adviser, the one Prophet Isaiah – spoke about (Isaiah 40: 13-14). I've realised with time, experience and practice that God, in fact, always answers prayers. I've also experienced that we must pray according to his will and not just our desires alone, if we want answers to our prayers. If our desires do not align with his will and purpose, we can be rest assured that our prayer will be answered either by his silence, delay, or denial.

As I progressed in my prayer life, I've also come to understand that it is more about developing and nourishing my relationship with him. It's no longer about what I want from him, but rather, a recognition, total dependence, and submission to who he is in my life. It is best expressed as coming into his presence, it's an invitation that comes from within and this for me, changes everything.

Prayer for me has two different perspectives. The first is when I ask God to listen to me. The second is when, on the contrary, I listen to God. Both have two different outcomes.

When I listen to God, to allow him to speak to my heart, I am drawn to remember and ponder the myriad of good things he has done for me. When I empty my thoughts and willingly submit myself to listen to Him, I am filled with nothing but gratitude for the past and no absolute fear or concern for the present or future.

But when I, on the contrary want God to listen to me, my focus shifts from all the good things he has done for me in the immediate and remote past, and I focus on the present or the future, on what he is yet to do for me. I have discovered that an important part of my communication with God is when I open up to listen to him and being reminded through gratitude, I am all the more confident to believe that if he did it before, he will surely do it again.

Prayer, above all, is worship – "hallowed be your name" is the first component of the Lord's Prayer. This is far from being coincidental. Prayer is first and foremost a call to sanctify, reverence, respect, consecrate and bless God who is himself Spirit and whoever worships him must do so in spirit and in truth (Jn 4:24). Worshipping God in truth simply means there is no lie or deception in us. I'm surprised at how easily we have discarded sin and assume that we can come boldly into his presence. Isaiah admonishes us to "wash, take your wrong doing out of my sight (Isaiah 1:16-17). The Psalmist tells us who can stand before the presence of the Lord. It is the man with clean hands and pure heart. (Ps 24:3-4). To have cleans hands means they are not stained with the blood of sin. Sometimes we assume that we have no sins because we have not directly or individually 'committed' any. But what about our participation as 'accessories' in the sins of others, by counsel, command, consent, provocation, praise or flattery, concealment, partaking, silence and by defense of the ill done?

A pure heart also means it is undefiled by inordinate passions and desires. I've come to recognise that the only way we can have clean hands and a pure heart is to live in obedience to his will and commandments. As Christians we often hold on to the promises of God and forget the applicable terms and conditions. Every promise is preceded by a condition. We leave out the 'if' and expect the 'then'.

My spiritual progress has developed hand in hand with my fellowship with the Holy Spirit. One thing I've come to understand is that while the grace of our Lord Jesus Christ and the love of God are freely given to us even without our asking or meriting them, fellowship of the Holy Spirit must be sent or given through request and desire, and then received (Lk 11:13, Acts 1:18, Jn 14:26, Jn 20:22). Fellowship with the Holy Spirit means communion, friendship, partnership, companionship or mutuality.

My favourite references to the power of the Holy Spirit at work in my life are – For God has not given us the spirit of fear (2Tm 1:7). In my book, *The Changing Landscape of Christianity in Africa*, I documented how being a "born again Catholic" and a "Catholic with a difference" helped me to conquer fear, once and for all after a near-death experience while traveling in a car in Nigeria. This was on the 15th of August 2007. Since then, I have never again experienced fear, such as the fear of my own death or the future.

Another scripture citation that has always worked for me, with me and through me is "but the Comforter whom the father will send in my name, he shall teach you all things and make you remember all things (Jn 14:26).

I can categorically say, without any iota of doubt that I'm a witness of how the Holy Spirit makes us remember 'all' things and not just some things. Although I have always enjoyed a very active memory and reminiscing ability, I'm sometimes a victim of distraction and absentmindedness. Most recently, I find myself, often forgetting where my car is parked in the busy supermarket. In these instances, simple steps, such as the practice of mindfulness or deliberateness have aided me.

Nevertheless, the Spirit prompts and reminds me of the important things I need to remember. For example, in February 2020, I had prepared my presentation for a book review, only to find out that what I had prepared to say had been said by speakers before me. We all knew the author's journey from the same perspective. So, it was only natural that we would all pick similar or same things to highlight about him and his book. I didn't panic when it was time for me to speak. I simply invited the Holy Spirit to speak in my place.

"Can I have your script"? The author came to ask me at the end. He was surprised when I said, "I don't have one". He went a step further to ask me to write down what I just said. Under normal circumstances, I would have been able to repeat my script word for word. But I knew this time was different. I had no idea because the entire presentation had not been done by me but only through me. I have no doubt who it was.

20

On Aloneness

There are two undeniable facts. We came alone into this world and we will leave alone. Anything in between, which we call life and how we live it is entirely subjective and a question of individual choice and responsibility.

As human beings, we tend to think that being alone, necessarily is to be unhappy. Cultural norms, traditions and societal expectations socialise us to believe that we must surround ourselves with people for us to be truly happy. This is particularly the case with the African concept of the society or community, where the individual is almost inexistent and individualism is defined in terms of belonging to a group and relationship to others. In this case, women, for example are recognised in the society by virtue of their roles and relationships as wives and mothers.

As a contributor to the initial debate of the existence of African Philosophy in Rome in the early 90s, I remember and pondered how the *cogito ergo sum*, (I think therefore I am) of Rene Descartes became "I am because we are and since we are, therefore I am" as the African representation of this philosophical thought on rationalism as a defining feature of individualism.

In traditional African context, a man is considered old enough to marry when he needs a woman to cook for him because his mother can no longer do so. Similarly, a young girl is socialised to consider marriage as an absolute priority in her bucket list.

Marriages, relationships or being always together is not an antidote to loneliness. With companionship in a formalised relationship comes the expectation of others being responsible for our happiness.

Aloneness is not about solitude or social isolation. The latter has become a cause for concern as a health hazard associated with prolonged loneliness. More recently, researchers have started calling for a public health approach to social isolation which they consider not only harmful to health but also come with the risk of early death by 26%. This is the same risk as smoking 15 cigarettes a day and greater risk of developing depression, dementia, heart disease and obesity. This simply means that people must connect with others to survive. How did we survive the restrictions imposed during the Covid 19 pandemic? Lockdown, traveling restrictions, social distancing, stay at home, stay alert and so on were introduced as our latest lingo with the new normal, which we seemed to have forgotten so soon. We were able to live without visiting friends and families for almost two years. Most people even lived without jobs, entertainment, football, parties, weddings and funerals. With the current stage of living with or rather ignoring the virus, despite new spikes and hikes of new and more infectious variants, we are now too busy dealing with other emergencies such as the ever-rising cost of living and loving, loneliness, mental health, food scarcity and security, energy poverty and much more.

The lesson I've learnt from most recent development across the world is that we are constantly being reminded of the need to go back to the basics and take individual responsibility for our lifestyle and other choices we make. We did not need spiralling cost of energy to decide whether to eat or heat or steal to eat in justification of pre-existing pilfering habits. We have lived and continue to live with too much when much less is required. We also surround ourselves with too many people when we have not even learnt how to live with ourselves. I've come to understand that the only person I will live with for the rest of my life is me. The ability to live with myself is a pre-requisite for my ability to live with another or others.

Aloneness, on the contrary, is the deliberate ability to cultivate and practice being alone with the self, without necessarily filling up time and space with people and things, whether they exist or not. I started practising and learning how to be alone by myself and with myself when I was supposedly surrounded with people. I learnt how to enjoy my own company and have meaningful and constructive conversations with myself. Becoming skilled at how to be alone with myself helped me through the lockdown restrictions. I was already familiar with being "locked up", so a "lockdown" was a no brainer for me.

In practising aloneness, it is vital to integrate silence as a virtue and value. We live in a very noisy world, so it can be difficult to eliminate the external noise in our environment and almost hear our own heartbeat. However challenging this practice may seem, there are vital benefits in incorporating silence into our daily routine. Silence has enabled me to become a better listener. It has also aided my observational skills which have enabled me to identify opportunities and details that others would ignore. In silence, I am able to eliminate every form of distraction, concentrate, avoid impulsive actions and most importantly, manage my expectations.

In cultivating silence, I have become more resilient, adaptable and flexible to new and developing situations which would, otherwise, have overwhelmed me. Most importantly, it is in silence that the Spirit speaks to me, drops ideas into my mind, lead me in the way that I should go and prompts me to pray when I don't know what words to use. Like the Prophet Elijah, I have learnt that the Lord is neither in the strong wind, earthquake or fire. He is in the still small voice (1 Kings 19: 12) which can only be heard in the silence of the heart and mind.

In life, I've heard, listened to and followed the directions indicated to me by different voices, often conflicting. With time, I have not only learnt how to listen to, but also to recognise that unique voice of the Holy Spirit. I have heard so many wrong voices, so I can recognise the right voice speaking to me. This has come gradually, through experiences and difficult times and a tried and tested approach to discernment.

21

On Christianity and Its Open Enemies

I am deeply concerned about the Christianity legacy we will leave for the future generations. I was born and brought up as a Catholic. Being a Christian for me, has, unequivocally meant being a Catholic. I must admit that although I may not have found all the answers to my existential questions, I have, through the Catholic Church and tradition, discovered where to look for them.

I marvel at the fact that it was the gentiles, or unbelievers who, in Antioch first referred to the followers of Jesus Christ as Christians (Acts 11:26). This was due to the constancy and consistency with which the early Christians met and taught people about Christ. Christians have always been persecuted and Jesus himself warned the apostles about this beforehand. In the beatitudes, Jesus says blessed or happy are you when people insult you, persecute you and say all false things against you because of me... (Matt 5: 11). The persecution of Christians sounds politically correct as they stand against everything the world stands for.

To be a Christian is not for the faint-hearted. It needs discipline, discipleship, integrity and the consistent and conscious choice of good over evil, even when the evil choice is more desirable and pleasurable. One of my favourite landmarks in Rome is the Colosseum. Each time I visited, I was reminded of the price Christians had to pay for their steadfast faith, even to accepting death in unimaginable ways, including being devoured alive by animals to the excitement and entertainment of others. Each time I also asked myself if I would be the Christian I claim to be today, if such sacrifices experienced by Christians in the past were required of me.

Secular culture is resistant of the authentic teachings of Christ because it finds it burdensome. This burden or 'yoke' of the Gospel is equally perceived by the younger generation as boredom.

Christ himself was and still is a sign of contradiction. His message of salvation and how this can be achieved is the same, yesterday, today, and forever. It cannot be updated like an app on our mobile phones, neither can it be interpreted to suit modern taste, varieties, and flavours. The Christian message is a difficult one. For this reason, many find it uncomfortable and look for the easy way out by compromising. Even in the time of Christ himself, many left because they found it difficult to follow him. To Jesus' question ... Simon Peter replied, "Lord to whom we shall go? You have the words of eternal life" (Jn 6:68).

St John reminds us that we can only claim to live in Christ if we live the same kind of life that he lived (1Jn 2:7).

The life in Christ is not a life of abundance in materialism. It is a contradiction in terms to claim that Christ renounced material comfort to encourage us to embrace it, that he became poor that we might be rich in the material things of this world. The wealth of a Christian is the very life of Christ himself. He is the Way, the Truth, and the Life (Jn 14:16)

The privilege that accompanies the life of believers goes with the honour to suffer for him (Phil 1:30). St Paul speaks of the need to share in the sufferings of Christ by reproducing the pattern of his death (Phil 3:11).

The life of a Christian is not necessarily full stomach and plenty but may also be empty stomach and poverty. It is inaccurate to preach that the life of a Christian is immune from challenges and lack. It is precisely through these challenges that we must bear witness to the message of salvation through faith and unconditional trust in divine providence.

Christians must constantly respond to the invitation of the teaching of the Master to strive to enter the narrow door (Lk 13:23). St. Matthew adds that the way that leads to perdition is wide and spacious, and many take it, but the narrow gate is a hard road that leads to life and only a few find it (Mt 7:13-14).

Christianity today is exposed to corruption and compromise, especially through the propagation of the gospel of prosperity proclaimed from the pulpits of unscrupulous professionals turned preachers. They sell misleading interpretations of the bible for profit without accountability. They base their teachings on some biblical facts devoid of contextualisation.

The main challenge today is that Churches are filled with Christians who feel they have given their lives to Christ but have not repented. We are in the face of a Christianity that is driven by emotion, feeds on emotion and instrumentalised by emotions. Sentimental Christians are also "Church Hoppers" or "Church Shoppers" who are constantly in search of places of worship where they feel "high", entertained and where they will not be reminded of the existence of their conscience or the hard message to remain in the straight and narrow.

Repentance or conversion on the other hand, is not an emotional or automatic response to stimuli. It is a decision which must involve the will and deliberate action to acknowledge inadequacy without God and to strive to seek to do what is right and just in the face of God and man.

Repentance is the beginning of a relationship with God, with the decision to break away from the past life of sin to embrace the new life in Christ. St Pauls in his letter to the Ephesians admonishes us to give up our old way of life, put aside the old self which gets corrupt by following illusory desires (Eph 4:22-24.). He also reminds us in Romans 12:2 "Do not model yourselves on the behaviour of the world around you, but let your behaviour change, modelled by your new mind. This is the only way to discover the will of God and know what is good, what it is that God wants, what is the perfect thing to do".

A major challenge we face today is the generation of young people who are constantly being fed with a distorted and monetised version of Christianity. There is the systematic replacement of religion with spirituality and the propagation of a spirituality devoid of a relationship with God. There is the general belief that "love is God", but this is not the same as "God is love". Young Christians today are devourers and followers of social media and technology. They take pleasure in how many "followers" they have, instead of being themselves followers of Jesus.

This poses another major threat in the face of an intruding AI (Artificial Intelligence) which is gradually taking control of our lives, changing our lifestyles and choices, and pushing our boundaries beyond the miraculous. Young and vulnerable people who are already isolated in real life and lack real human and family connections have transferred their abode to the virtual world, where they are made to believe in an inexistent connectedness with others. AI promises to deliver more and take the damages already done by social media to another level of isolation camouflaged for connections, create machines than not only think, act, behave and interact with us and for us but can even predict what we feel or think.

Without knowing it, we are heading towards more confusion, anarchy, and disillusionment. Facts and fictions can no longer be distinguished, one from the other. Are we heading towards a bible that will be completely written by AI? We are not that far away.

The belong, believe, and behave agenda of AI poses a serious cause for concern. The deep fake recreation of a digital and reimagined version, using voices and images to bring people back from the dead is worrisome. Digitally simulated resurrection can be used maliciously to validate misleading claims of miracles and controvert authentic identity of biblical sources.

Although Christian denominational pluralism and proliferation cannot be discounted, this ethnic-salad-bowl approach to Christianity will not be sustainable in the long run.

In the midst of this pillar to post approach to Christianity, there is need for a new evangelisation and a visitation of authentic Christian faith and values.

While the kaleidoscope of Christianity hangs in the tripartite scramble for money, membership and miracles, the Mother Church must adopt an innovative approach that goes beyond and above sermonisation, indoctrination and moral instruction to teaching the Word, and creating spaces, places and times for people to engage with their faith in ways that are meaningful, and reflective of their experiences and challenges in a world that is constantly changing. Those who freely choose to belong should be encouraged to truly believe and behave in a way that conforms to what they believe and where they belong.

A good place to start is the very beginning. The Catholic Church, as the Mother Church has the obligation to initiate or strengthen existing processes of internal evangelisation. Its main strength remains the propagation of the Word and Sacraments, especially that of the Holy Eucharist. Nevertheless, the scriptural foundations on which the sacraments, traditions and magisterium are anchored appear not to be emphasised enough, as many Catholics don't seem to know and appreciate what they have in the salvific grace of the sacraments.

Despite current and future developments in Christianity and its open enemies which legitimate the qualification as a kingdom divided against itself, I strongly believe in the words of Jesus, the Christ:

"You are Peter and on this rock I will build my Church.

And the gates of the underworld can never hold out against it" (Matt 16:18).

Maranatha.

PART IV

ANNOTATED PUBLICATIONS

Human Trafficking in Nigeria 1960–2020: Pattern, People, Purpose, and Places (2023) Edited by Pauline Aweto, Akinyinka Akinyoade and Francesco Carcedi, African Studies Centre, Leiden Netherlands.

Since the "migration crisis" in Europe exceeded its maximum tolerance level in 2015, more than 18,000 Africans have died crossing the Mediterranean Sea, according to the reports of the United Agency for Migration, the International organisation for Migration (IOM). Similarly, according to the reports of another agency of the UN, the United Nations High Commission for Refugees (UNHCR), the year 2019 is the 6th consecutive year that the "bleak milestone" of 1,000 deaths per annum has been recorded.

While both agencies are quick to cautiously specify that their data are strictly on minimum estimate basis, due to the obvious fact that many go unrecorded, it goes without saying therefore, that it would no longer be business as usual to blame the ill fate or misadventure of these "underserving" Africans, who have either remained buried in the deep Mediterranean, or have earned foreign graves as unmerited trophies after losing their lives, in a dangerously daunting attempt to find new and better ones: The one they were never to have.

Since then, issues of migration from Africa, especially to Europe have become more than ever polarised, thanks especially to media. Consequently, previous researchers have, disconnectedly and intermittently sought to deconstruct and reconstruct this media misconception alongside misrepresentation of African migration in Europe.

This current research comes as a child of its time. With 16 African countries, reaching the 60 years milestone of independence in 2020, there is no better time than now, to seize this unique opportunity to significantly explore and reopen the debate on African migration, within and across African countries, and to Europe with country focus on Nigeria, alongside the complex intersectionality of illegal migration, economic migration, smuggling and human trafficking.

"Human Trafficking, Modern Day Slavery and Global Public Health: The Impact of Covid 19 and the "New Normal" on Old Narratives" in Human Trafficking in Nigeria 1960-2020: Pattern, People, Purpose, and Places (2023) Edited by Pauline Aweto, Akinyinka Akinyoade and Francesco Carcedi, African Studies Centre, Leiden Netherlands.

The World Health Organisation (WHO) defines public health as 'the art and science of preventing disease, prolonging life and promoting health through the organised efforts of society' Understood from this perspective, it could reasonably be argued that a specific public health approach, which focuses on preventive measures, inclusive of health promotion, has, to a significant extent, been absent in existing measures to tackle the scourge of human trafficking and/or modern-day slavery. Therefore, this chapter aims to establish the tripartite framework and triangular relationship of interdependence between human trafficking, modern-day slavery and global public health. Nevertheless, the most recent Covid 19 pandemic has become a major game changer which legitimates global health's focus on non-communicable diseases and will, for a long time to come, shape the content of concern, where human movement, migration, and, by extension, human trafficking and modern-day slavery cannot but constitute an essential part of a conversation that has, excessively been long overdue.

"Cultural Competence in Health Promotion Initiatives for Nigerian Victims of Human Trafficking" Parma, 23rd February, and 9th March 2022.

Food culture preference is one of the traditions that migrants find difficult to abandon in their processes of integration into the new culture of their host country. It is a way of preserving individual as well as the group's cultural values and identities for them to feel at home away from home. The central role played by food in the Nigerian culture as care, community, culture, communication, and ceremony are underlined alongside the use of health belief and behaviour change models of health promotion.

"Strengthening Human Capacity against Human Trafficking in the Covid Era (the virus, the variants and the vaccine)" Keynote address delivered to leaders at the international symposium organised by Talitha Kum Rome and the Pontifical Salesian University, Rome, Italy. 5th March 2021(online).

This address introduces how the use of words such as 'social distancing', 'social isolation', self-isolation, lockdown, stay at home, stay alert, travel bans, and restriction have not only transmuted social consciousness but also introduced new challenges to fighting the scourge of human trafficking. Ironically, the common platform of the new normal, exposes and creates other forms of inequalities, inequities, and disparities.

The pandemic also exposes and accentuates "underlying conditions" of vulnerability, including poverty, lack of access to education, domestic violence, an unending litany of traditions which promotes a culture of violence, silence, and stigma. This address shares evidence from the global report on human trafficking by the United nation's Office for Drugs and Crime (UNDC:2020) to confirm that the most common form of human trafficking is sexual exploitation (79%), that "women trafficking women is the norm" (a war of women against women) and that, contrary to our perception of human trafficking, which necessarily involved international movements, the report confirms that "most exploitation takes place close home" (UNODC:2020).

It is recommended that there is need to address and discourage demands that foster exploitation that leads to human trafficking: education and lack of access, shift in values, traditions, and culture that promote gender inequality, silence, and stigma. The address also called for a focus shift from formal education to skills acquisition/entrepreneurship/apprenticeship, harnessing the underutilized skills of informal education cemented in the experience African women acquire in life in their traditional roles as wives and mothers. It concludes with the call to a new way of evangelisation, underlining 2 major features of the new normal – First, technology which is significantly replacing transportation and transfer, which are determinants of the Palermo Protocol's definition of human trafficking. Secondly, there is a whole generation of young people with a distorted version of Christianity: This is the main challenge pre and post Covid 19.

"Online Education and its potential for female empowerment", Cambridge Centre for Applied Research on Human Trafficking (CCARHT: 2020).

One of the major areas that has significantly been affected by the "new normal" as a direct consequence of the Covid 19 pandemic is, without doubt, education, in all its ramifications. To some extent, although the virtual learning environment has been an essential part of both teaching and learning modes, the outbreak of the Covid 19 pandemic was a major game changer, as online teaching and learning, suddenly became, as a matter of necessity, the only choice, with no other options, especially at the initial stages of the pandemic, when scientists still grappled to understand the basic *modus operandi* of the virus and the world struggled to fight with an invisible enemy they knew nothing about. Nevertheless, although online learning as a forceful imposition by the pandemic equally ushered in new empowerment opportunities, such as breaking geographical barriers and personal constraints to study on a global platform of convergence, on the other hand, this "new normal", ironically, not only creates but more importantly exposes and highlights existing forms of inequalities and educational disparities. This paper aims to interrogate the sustainability of SDG4 (Sustainable Development Goal 4) on Quality Education and the challenges of online education delivery in the ongoing pandemic as well as its aftermath. It draws significantly from the specific experiences of Black and Ethnic Minority adult women, who are currently pursuing a degree programme in the United Kingdom. It navigates between the opportunities for women empowerment alongside challenges of online education in the context of the Covid 19 Pandemic.

"The role of women as communication leads in the health sector of the ongoing new normal", The Nigerian Institute for Public Health, in collaboration with Global Alliance for Public Relations and Communications Management. 19th September 2020.

Starting with the new normal dilemma, which exposes health inequalities and disparities as well as underlying health conditions as a major contributory factor to outcomes in the instances of exposure to Covid 19, this presentation considers the "underlying Nigerian factor" which emphasises on health as the absence of illness and not overall wellbeing. It draws attention to how we look, how we appear and not how we feel and even when we focus on how we feel, it is on how people make us feel or how we should feel. It attempts to find explanations in African traditional life, where the individual does not and cannot exist alone except corporately.

While the global community attempt global solutions to the Covid 19, it is of vital importance that Nigeria does not just duplicate, copy, or import some of these global responses without first addressing its specifically "underlying" local conditions in order to make any relevance in the global arena. To do this, it would be relevant to look at what is practicable and applicable to the Nigerian environment alongside its culture, ways of being and doing, traditions and unparalleled gender roles. In conclusion, focus on health promotion and the prevention of illnesses/ diseases is recommended alongside a shift from formal education to harnessing the underutilised skills of informal education cemented in the experience women acquire in life in their roles as wives, mothers, and care givers.

"The Nigerian Diaspora: Trafficking of Nigerian Women for Sexual Exploitation in Europe and Italy", Catanzaro, Italy. 25/26 September 2018.

With different arguments, this paper presents analytical points of reflection on the dynamics and evolution of the underlying processes of the impact of migration, on both origin and destination countries. Discussion centers around the visible results and effectiveness of counter-trafficking activities in support of Nigerian victims of human trafficking across 25 years of practice to further explore changes of the phenomenon itself, recruitment strategies, models of exploitation and liberation. It further addresses the differences between trafficking of African women to Italy and the United Kingdom, highlights differences in the use of terminologies, for example human trafficking for sexual exploitation (Italy) or modern-day slavery (UK), considers implications, scope of support and challenges. In a specific manner, it reflects on some good practices from the UK, such as the National Referral Mechanism (NRM) and the Modern- day Slavery Act 2015 and their implications for current and future practice in the protection of the victims of human trafficking/modern-day slavery.

"Nigerian culture, traditions, and gender-based Violence", Parma, 27th September 2017.

"Prevention and Counter trafficking of Nigerian Women" conference, Parma, 6th April 2016.

This paper considers gender-based violence as weapon of war and peace, highlighting some naturally occurring instances in the Nigerian culture and traditional perspective of women which provide the breeding ground for violence against women. In a specific manner, it looks at the interconnection between cultural practices and gender-based violence.

The Sound of Silence (2015), Authorhouse UK, USA.

A compelling story of conflict between the forces of faith and fate. Joy's greatest nightmare became a reality when she came face to face with the tragic lies, crime and deceit behind the veil of the empty promises of a better life in Europe. Exactly how far is she ready to defy her plight and dare to be different? Will she make up her mind, for the last time, to embrace what had timelessly been revealed as her true destiny from which she could no longer run away?

"Nigeria: Boko Haram and Gender-Based Violence as War Weapon" in Stupri di Guerra e violenze di genere edited by Simona La Rocca (2015) Ediesse, Rome.

This paper interrogates gender-based violence on the platform of the abduction of the Chibok girls in 2014. Relying substantially on the evidence documented by Human Rights Watch on the types of violence meted out on the girls, including physical and psychological violence, forced labour, domestic work and participation in military operation as 'baits', it is argued that there is a qualitative leap from the consideration of women as weapon of peace to highlight their active role as war weapon – an emerging reality that defies the changing traditional role of women.

"Coming out of the silence of violence" (Interview with Alicia Lopes Araujo, published in L'Osservatore Romano, donne Chiesa mondo August – September 2013

To mark the 50th anniversary of the foundation of the African Union (formally, Organisation for African Unity) this interview discusses the journey so far in addressing the condition of women in Africa. It focuses on themes highlighted in the book, Wartime Rape, African Values at Crossroads (2010).

The Changing Landscape of Christianity in Africa, (2012) Paulines Publication, Africa.

While every age has its own distortion of Christianity, the distortion of Christianity in our time is the preaching of the "Gospel of Prosperity", and at the heart of this Gospel is the teaching that the material things one asks of God are more important than God himself. Some go to Church, not in search of God but in search of riches, husband, wife, children, promotion, or even a visa. It is the pure, unrestricted but well-ordered desire for the truth, which this book represents that we find God, or rather, that we allow God to find us. And, having allowed ourselves to be found by God, we can find ourselves (From Foreword by Most Rev. Felix Alaba Job, Archbishop of Ibadan, Nigeria, now, Emeritus).

Lo stupro come arma di Guerra in Africa (2012) l'Hamattan Italia, Torino

This is the Italian version of Wartime Rape, African Values at Crossroads (2010) Ambassador Publications, Nigeria.

"Stop Violence against African Women" (exclusive interview with Stephen Ogongo Ongong'a, Editor, Africa News Italy and Germany, 5th May 2011.

Many aspects of African cultures seem to tolerate if not promote violence against women. A new book titled "Wartime rape: African values at Crossroads by Dr Pauline Aweto Eze explores some of these elements within African cultures that continue to perpetrate violence against women and how this is further instrumentalised and worsened during conflicts and crisis. The book is a call to reflection on these attitudes and practices, and a challenge to stop all forms of violence against women.

Wartime Rape; African Values at Crossroads, (2010) Ambassador Publications, Nigeria.

The book is a call to introspection. The author uses the theme of rape as weapon of war as a motif to gather together a number of related and urgent issues: violence and war, different types of abuse, Africa and its traditional values, media propaganda, the HIV and AIDS drama, rape, publicity and humiliation. She swoops between the various manifestations of violence against women both in the times of war and in moments of relative peace. The core interest revolves around the use of rape as weapon in the context of African wars. However, the research also delves into what the author presents as African traditional wars against women. (Foreword, Msgnr Fortunatus Nwachukwu, Chief of Protocol, Secretariat of State, Vatican City, Rome, now Archbishop Fortunatus Nwachukwu, Permanent Observer of the Holy See to the United Nations, Geneva).

"Present dilemma and future perspettive: The Nigerian experience" (2009) in Rapporto annuale del sistema di protezione per richiedenti asilo e rifugiati, Rome, Italy, S.T.R. p.157-179.

In this contribution to the annual report on the system of protection of refugees and asylum seekers, the paper underlines the dialectic and dilemma of the 'push factors' (people smugglers, traffickers, vulnerability of victims and lack of employment opportunities in country of origin) as well as the pull factors, where most arrivals on the coast of Italy do so by chance (considering Italy's geographical location in the Mediterranean Sea) and not by choice. The focus shifts to the experiences of women, victims of trafficking and their experiences of violence which legitimate their application for protection in the host country.

"African Trafficking; It Cannot Stand" (2007) in C. Pemberton et al (eds), Not for Sale, Raising Awareness, Fighting Exploitation, Great Britain, Inspire, p.12-14.

Trafficking in human lives is generally defined as the slave trade of the twenty-first century. It is often implied that slave trade, in all forms and expressions, has long been abolished. This is not the case. Rather than a reoccurrence, the sad picture is that of permanence and perpetuation of the phenomenon. This is particularly pertinent to some

African cultures and traditions, whose regimes have fuelled and instigated the subjection and exploitation of women. They have also contributed heavily to the supply chain in the international market of sex slavery.

By virtue of their exclusion from 'unnecessary' education, these women are to be eternally cared for and protected by men who can possess them as properties or 'personal items', bought and paid for, as it were.

Poverty is the main cause or 'push factor' of trafficking. Another major, profound root cause is globalisation, particularly the absurd, pacific coexistence of poverty and opulence. Religion and religious beliefs constitute an essential element in the trafficking of African women. Some new Churches have implemented selective reading of the Bible which encourages false hopes. They convince believers that material wealth goes hand in hand with faith and is a right, owed to them by God, which they are entitled to claim. These Churches, in simple terms, preach that the end justifies the means: dispensing with conscience and the sense of sin. There are also instances where Church leaders misuse their positions. Addressing the issue of gender equality in African countries constitutes a vital milestone in the global fight against trafficking. Given the huge role played by African women in the entire process and procedure of trafficking, the situation could rightly be defined as a kingdom divided against itself. It cannot stand.

"Identity and Change in African Culture; The Case of African women" (2005) in J. O. Oguejiofor and G. O. Onah (eds), African Philosophy and the Hermeneutics of Culture, Essays in Honour of Theophilus Okere, Studies in African Philosophy, Munster, Germany, Lit Verlag, p. 277-296.

A reflection on the changing identity and roles of African women pre and post-colonial times as well as current and future challenges facing women in the continent. It also looks at the implication of their non-representation and exclusion from politics and recommends education as the point of departure.

"African Women in Intercultural Perspettive" (2004a) in F. Brezzi and G. Providenti (eds), Spostando I mattoni a mani nude, Milan, Italy, Franco Angeli, p. 180-186.

This contributory chapter considers the identity and role of African women in the processes of migration and interculture, alongside problems associated with integration in their host country. It focuses particularly on the trafficking of women for sexual exploitation and modern-day slavery.

"Checks and Balances in African Philosophy" (2004b) in F. Lopez (ed), Philosophy without Fetishism, Milan, Italy, Edizioni Associate, pp 82-92.

This chapter looks at the identity of African women as wives and mothers, offering insight and some philosophical implications and limitations.

"Engendering Government and Leadership in Africa; A Philosophical Inquiry" (2003) in J.O.Oguejiofor (ed), Philosophy, Democracy and Responsible Governance in Africa, Munster, Germany, Lit Verlag, p. 481-493.

The underlying intention of this paper is the proposal of a gender-conscious leadership, calling for the appropriation of feminine values, principles, and qualities, irrespective of whether such leaders are male or female. A re-visitation of Plato's philosophical ideas on leadership shows that his Philosopher –King could as well be a Philosopher – Queen. It is argued that this idea may be too mature or premature for the African mind, especially for the African woman herself, who may be the only insurmountable obstacle towards the realisation of such ideal.

"Trafficking – Focus on West Africa", Bolzano 6th December 2002.

Focuses on the evolution, trafficking, especially of Nigerian women and girls, socio-economic and political background, condition of women in Nigeria, specific modality of trafficking, prostitution, possible solutions and exit strategies.

"Secularisation of Western Culture in the Philosophy of Nietzsche; The African Response" (2001) in L. Arcella (ed), Friedrich Nietzsche; Oltre l'occidente, Rome, Italy, settimo sigillo, p.201-215.

This paper navigates through the development of the philosophical thoughts of Fredrick Nietzsche, climaxing in his proclamation of the death of God in his *Thus Spake Zarathustra*. Proposing an African response, the central thesis is that the death of god is the natural consequence of the western concept of a god that is impersonal, transcendent and secularised. On the contrary, the African traditional concept presents 'experience at the centre of a non-mediated concept of god, who does not dance alone but with his people. Central in this paper is the leap from the concept of the 'people of god' to 'God of the people'.

"Women in African Thought" (2000) in L. Processi (ed), Prospects of African Philosophy, University of Rome, Romatre, Rome, p.107-120.

It is inevitable to include women in the conversation on the promotion of intercultural knowledge and interaction, especially as this is conspicuously absent in the debate on African philosophical thoughts. This paper therefore, highlights the philosophy of Herbert Marcuse on women's liberation, oscillating between the dilemma of 'destructive productivity, and the 'masculine principle' as well as the revolutionary role of women in the transformation of advanced industrial societies, as proposed in his *One Dimensional Man.*

"North African Feminism" (2000) in The Rutledge International Encyclopaedia of Women; Global Women's Issues and Knowledge, New York, vol. 2, p.803-807.

This contributory chapter defines feminism as essentially conditioned and characterised by cultural, historical, traditional, political, and socio-economic factors. It evaluates the uniqueness of North African Feminism between Arab tradition and culture on the one hand and Islamic fundamentalism on the other, while considering a brief excursus through the historical development and participation of women as well as their contribution pre and post-independence period. It analyses key campaigns and feminist movements and some major achievements, including and not limited to marginal political participation and mobilisation in fighting alongside men for the liberation of their countries. It concludes with a proposal of education, not only for North African women but for women globally and particularly for women in the developing countries. Until the problem of female mass illiteracy is addressed, feminism, liberation and emancipation will continue to remain an elitist issue as it is currently.

"What is left of the Law of immigration for Women?" in 'il foglio del paese delle donne' (a women's weekly), year X, no. 43, 8ᵗʰ October, 1997, p.3.

A very vocal and provocative reaction to the Italian government's decision to exclude the right to vote for foreigners from the newly designed law on immigration. As the title suggests there is nothing left in a law on immigration that denies or excludes their rights to vote.

"Nigerian Petroleum Kills Hope", Il manifesto, via Tomacelli 146, 00186 Roma

This argues in support of the violation of human rights associated with the killing of the Nigerian activist, Ken Saro Wiwa and the suspension of Nigeria from the Commonwealth by the United Nations.

"Educating the African Woman: An experience of Integration" (1996) in Dossier di scuola e intercultura, Bologna, Italy, 20th January, p.12-13.

This is a testimonial of experience of being a black African woman in Italy, exploring the benefits of formal and informal education and the challenges of promoting intercultural dialogue and integration of African women. It underlines the need to promote mutual knowledge, dialogue, tolerance and peaceful co-existence amidst emerging issues and dilemma of the integration of migrant children in Italian schools.

"Women's Role in the Promotion of Life and Peace" (1995a) in educare una donna e' educare un popolo, September 1995, p. 16-17.

Based on the general theme of this annual programme, by the Asmara missionary group, "To educate a woman is to educate a nation", this article reflects on the current role, identity and status of African women as wives and mothers as they promote life and contribute to maintaining peace. It underlines the need to go beyond mass female literacy projects to a more structured and formalised system of educating the girl child as a priority for African countries

"Black Rain" (1995b) in il manifesto (national newspaper), year XXV, no. 272, Friday, 17th November 1995, p.21.

"Thoughts on the role of the African Woman" (1994) in Amici della scuola, year XXXI, no.4, September 1994.

"African Women between Tradition and Modernity" (1994) in Amicizia, year XXXI, no.3.

Though recognising similarities in the experiences of African women, this article focuses on the conditions of Nigerian women. It reflects on their identity amidst different political, social, cultural, religious and traditional factors which contribute to the subjection and exclusion of women. It concludes with a note of optimism in the potential of women in the new millennium, encouraging women to embrace their emerging role in society as universally defined. To do this, the education of the African gild child is recommended as the non-negotiable point of departure.

"God in African Religious Experience" (1992) in 'The Planetary Turn of God; From the Religious to the Secular experience of God', Rome, Borla,

This article focuses on African traditional concepts of God as distinctly different from those of Christianity and Islam, especially on African religious experience, the totality of life, origin, destiny, and the interconnection between the sacred and profane.

Man in the Technological Society: The Marcusean Utopia to overcome Alienation (1992), Doctoral Thesis, Rome, Italy.

A quarter-century after the publication of Herbert Marcuse's most polemic book, One Dimensional Man: Studies in the ideology of Advanced Industrial Society (1964), the general situation is a confirmation of the return of One Dimensional Man and one dimensionality. Various forms and figures of *"blockierte gessellschaft"* on the political and cultural levels continue to be part of our existence, as equally authoritarian and totalitarian regimes succeed one another. We continue to submit to the peaceful production of the means of destruction as the recent wars in the Gulf verifies. False needs are continually created by the mass media and advertisement which in turn continue to play into the hands of the powers that be. Despite our heightened level of attained civilisation and culture, the individual continues to remain negated and alienated. Wars, automation, unemployment, racism, masochism, sadism, existential frustration, poverty, brutality and drug use and abuse continue to be part of our everyday societal existence. As Marcuse would say, these are no instances of "relapse into barbarism" but the unrepressed implementation of the achievements of modern science and technology.

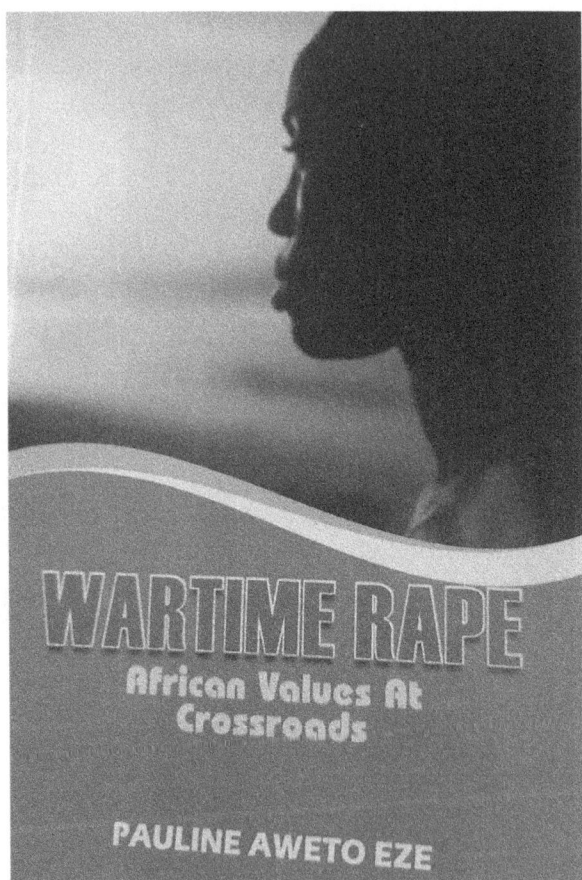

WARTIME RAPE

African Values At
Crossroads

PAULINE AWETO EZE

THE CHANGING LANDSCAPE
OF **CHRISTIANITY
IN AFRICA**

Pauline Aweto Eze

Paulines

Pauline Aweto

The Sound of Silence

PONTIFICAL SALESIAN UNIVERSITY
FACULTY OF PHILOSOPHY

Doctoral Thesis N° 289

AWETO OGHO PAULINE

MAN IN THE TECHNOLOGICAL SOCIETY;
THE MARCUSEAN UTOPIA TO OVERCOME ALIENATION

Extract from Doctoral Dissertation
in the Faculty of Philosophy

ROME, 1992

Glossary

Cogito ergo sum (Latin) I think therefore I am.

Mea colpa (Latin): An acknowledgement of one's own fault or mistake.

Oyinbo (Nigerian Pidgin English) A person of European descent.

Via crucis (Latin) The way or stations of the cross.

Mysterium et fascinans. (Latin) Fearful and fascinating.

Te Deum (Latin) God we praise you. A traditional Latin hymn of rejoicing.

Natale con i tuoi, pasqua con chi vuoi (Italian) Spend Christmas with your family and Easter with whoever you wish.

Presidente della repubblica (Italian) President of the Republic.

Lenticchie (Italian) Lentils.

Questo non e' per te (Italian) This is not for you.

Donne intelettuale africane (Italian) African Intellectual Women.

Un posto fisso (Italian) A permanent position.

Precarieta (Italian) Precariousness.

Parmegiano Reggiano (Italian) Name of Italian cheese.

Contra naturam (Latin) Against nature.

In vino veritas (Latin) In wine there is truth.

Haba.

Disgusto (Italian) Repulsion.

Wahala (Nigerian Pidgin English) Trouble, worry.

Nur um dem hofungnsloss haben uns Hoffnung gegeben"
(German) It is only for the sake of those without hope that
hope is given to us (Walter Adorno).

Che tempi ragazzi! (Italian) What a time!

*Ti voglio tanto bene mamma (*Italian) I love you mum.

Tenui Nec Dimittam (Latin) I have hold of you and I will not
let you go.

Pace in terra agli uomini, di buona volontà (Italian) Peace
to men of goodwill.

Bulala (Nigerian) Cane.

babbo natale. Esiste ancora? Ma certo che esiste (Italian)
Father Christmas, does he still exist? Certainly.

Fine. E vissero felici e contenti (Italian) The end. And they
lived happily ever after.

About the Author

Pauline Aweto holds a PhD from the Pontifical Salesian University, Rome, Italy. She has written extensively and contributed to research and publications on gender, including "North African Feminism" in the Routledge International Encyclopedia of Women: Global Women's Issues and Knowledge. She is also the author of the books, The Sound of Silence, Wartime Rape: African Values at Crossroads, and The Changing Landscape of Christianity in Africa.

She is actively involved in the socio-cultural integration of trafficked women in Italy. She was an invited lecturer to the Third University of Rome, Romatre, and was for four years a permanent member of the European Project: Equity and Difference across and within European Countries, Training for a Culture of Difference.

She was a Consultant with the International Organisation for Migration (IOM) within the Programme of the Assisted Voluntary Return and Reintegration of the Victims of Human Trafficking for Sexual Exploitation.

Currently, she is a Senior Lecturer and Senior Fellow of the Higher Education Academy (SFHEA). She lives in London and has two sons, Chris, and Ken, and two granddaughters, Phoenix, and Aurora.